Vicesimus Knox

## A Narrative of Transactions Relative to a Sermon

Preached in the Parish Church of Brighton, August 18, 1793

Vicesimus Knox

**A Narrative of Transactions Relative to a Sermon**
*Preached in the Parish Church of Brighton, August 18, 1793*

ISBN/EAN: 9783744746557

Printed in Europe, USA, Canada, Australia, Japan

Cover: Foto ©Lupo / pixelio.de

More available books at **www.hansebooks.com**

# A NARRATIVE
## OF
## TRANSACTIONS
### RELATIVE TO A
# SERMON,

PREACHED IN THE

Parish Church of *Brighton*, August 18, 1793:

WITH

Short EXTRACTS from the SERMON,

AND

OCCASIONAL REMARKS.

---

By VICESIMUS KNOX, D.D.
MASTER OF TUNBRIDGE SCHOOL, AND LATE FELLOW
OF ST. JOHN's COLLEGE, OXFORD.

---

" —— Stirpem et genus omne futurum
" Exercete odiis : ——
" —— Nullus amor populis, nec foedera sunto :
" Littora littoribus contraria, fluctibus undas,
" IMPRECOR, arma armis, pugnent IPSIQUE NEPOTESQUE !!!!
                                    *Haec Brightonius.*

---

LONDON:
PRINTED FOR C. DILLY, IN THE POULTRY.

# PROLEGOMENA.

To certain Persons UNKNOWN; but, in the *anonymous* Autography of their Requisition, Manifesto, or Mandate, directed and sent to Dr. KNOX in Brighton Theatre, denominating themselves, "THE GENTLEMEN OF "THIS THEATRE."

*Gentlemen of this Theatre,*

WHEN one man accosts another by name in the street, who has not the pleasure of knowing him, the man so accosted usually returns the civility of the hat, and says, "Sir, "you have the advantage of me." Upon my word, *Gentlemen of* THIS *Theatre*, I must confess that *you* have the advantage of *me*. I see indeed my own name on the back of the note which you did me the honour to send me; but, in the inside, I see no name at all, and can find no appellation with which to address you, but that which, in the note, you yourselves have thought proper to assume, *videlicet*, " THE GENTLEMEN OF THIS THEATRE." I never saw your faces before, and I have never heard your names since;—so that you most certainly have the advantage of me. *Non sumus ergo pares.—Impar congressus.—Do lubens manus.*

That point is very clear. I certainly do not know *who* you are; it remains to be decided *what* you are. Let me put on my spectacles, and look at your own manuscript note once more.—" *The—Gentlemen—*OF*—this—*" *Theatre;*"—OF this Theatre,—" OF,"—that is,—the Gentlemen OF or *belonging to* this Theatre.—Aye; there I have it, sure enough. The Gentlemen of this Theatre must be the PLAYERS; the Gentlemen of the Sock and Buskin, belonging to Brighton Theatre.———
" Your servant, Gentlemen; I like you too
" well to leave you yet.—*Pardonnez moi.*"

I take off my spectacles with the satisfaction of a man who has just made a discovery; and, turning them round and round with my finger, I turn the discovery in my thoughts at the same time.———No, no,—it will not do;—it cannot

cannot be so. The Gentlemen Players are gentlemen too well bred and too discreet, to turn out the spectators,—their customers,—quiet people too, who disturb nobody, and have just paid for five seats in the boxes.—Besides, you see "the Gentlemen of this "Theatre" are here close behind us,—coming along with their own letter themselves, like the Irishmen.—See, see, they are clad in *military uniform*;—they *cannot* be the Players; they are soldiers in *right earnest*.—Do observe their *uniform*.

"Pshaw!" say you, "for that matter, "and as to the military uniform, the Play-"ers, man, have all sorts of dresses; and "could furbish up a little company of sol-"diers, in the twinkling of an eye, out of "their theatrical wardrobe;—soldiers that "would look as well as these do, for the mat-"ter of *look*, if that's all, I warrant ye. They "need only call in those useful auxiliaries, at "a *pinch*, the candle-snuffers; or those gentle-"men that are so well skilled in manœu-"vring, the scene-shifters; and depend upon "it that is the case. There is no absolute "impossibility, but that these personages,

"though

" though in a subaltern sphere, may have
" styled themselves, with ambitious aspira-
" tion, " *The* Gentlemen *of* THIS *Theatre.*"

Very good, very good indeed!—This is a part of the *play* then;—excellent, i'faith; most excellent!—This is the "*Agreeable Surprise*" then, that was announced in the play-bill for to-night's amusement. I thought the *play* was over;—but there now lies the *surprise*;—it is *not* over,—this is the *sixth* act.—Well, the more for money the better. This is something *surprising* indeed; and prodigiously *agreeable*, I own: But I did not know that I was one of the *dramatis personæ*;—they should have acquainted me beforehand; I was quite ignorant of the plot:—but the *Gentlemen of this Theatre* have sent me directions, I suppose, in this billet. Well, let us read on.——Oh!—I see, I must go out; must not I?—I am but a *novice in theatricals*; but I am docile—willing to learn.—I see, by my instructions, I must go out *immediately*,—surrounded, I suppose, by my *life-guards*. Egad! I shall be as proud as an emperor, as I march through the narrow defile, lined on each side with janizaries, paying me obeisance!—

This

This is a mighty pretty play indeed: but I am in the dark—quite in the dark still—as to the *plot*; yet the prompter calls, and I must go. You, however, *Gentlemen of this Theatre*, have the goodness to give me my *cue*, and let me know what I am to do *next*. I am all compliance. Cannot the ladies here at my right hand perform any part in this *agreeable surprise?* I see they are following.—Bravo!—It will be a fine procession! it will have a rare effect!— Yet the worst of it is, *Gentlemen of this Theatre*, the audience cannot see what passes in this dismal lobby: but they will see bye and bye, I dare say.

Heyday!—What now?—You are very *noisy* methinks, *Gentlemen of this Theatre.*—What! are all those ill names, and all that foul language, in the play-book?—Are you sure you are right?—Do you proceed according to the book?—It cannot be. Why, I hear nothing but stark nonsense;—neither wit, nor humour, nor rhyme, nor reason;—downright vulgar scurrility and balderdash. If this be humour, it is both low humour and ill humour. The ladies and I do not chuse to act in so ill-chosen a play. For my own part, I think you must

have

have made some mistake; I am sure you are all acting out of your character.

Let me look at you once more. I wish there was more light in this passage. Good lack! if I see clearly, you are the very identical gentlemen whom I saw sitting, during the first five acts of the play, on the opposite side of the house, which, I observed, was nearly empty when we all set out in this procession: the very same, no doubt. I have a perfect remembrance of one gentleman's face; but I neither know his quality nor his name. All I know is, that these grand personages cannot be the *players*. I see how it is now. Their honours have purchased all the boxes for the season, or got a patent jurisdiction over the whole house; and so, though they do not, properly speaking, *belong to the Theatre*, as I too precipitately concluded from their calling themselves the *Gentlemen of this Theatre*, yet the *Theatre belongs to them*; aye, aye; and I have unfortunately intruded, without their permission, on what they call THEIR GROUND; that is, their freehold; whence they have a right to drive all others away, as the dog did from the manger. Ten thousand millions of pardons.

pardons do we all beg you, you kind, good, dear *Gentlemen of* this *Theatre*.—We saw the play advertised;—we paid our money at the door, and we were placed here by the box-keeper.—Excuse our ignorance,—we knew of no *exclusive* rights here:—and if we can presume to have equal rights with you at the Theatre, then *yours* was the intrusion into our company, not ours into yours,—for we were here before you. But, right or wrong, it is not worth contending about; for might overcomes right; and the might is all on your own side: *Contendere durum est, cum victore—sequor.*

" *Off, off.—Off, off,* Democrat.—*Off, off,*
" Sedition.—*Off, off,* Sermon."

Well, *Gentlemen of* this *Theatre*, we are retreating as fast as you will let us pass. We have been under a mistake. We did not know that you had exclusive rights, or that you could shew your commissions. We thought you merely players,—

That fret and strut their hour upon the stage,<br>
And then go off as well as we.

*Scribis cryptic, exeunt omnes!*

All

All this mistake now arose from your styling yourselves, "*The Gentlemen of this Theatre.*" Had you condescended to let us know your RIGHTS, or would have shewn us your commissions, it would have saved you from making your throats sore with calling us such hard names; and that gentleman yonder would not have been so much out of breath, and looked so pale. The ladies have *salts* in their pockets;—do let them administer them to his nose. He seems quite faint, poor gentleman. Well—Good night to you. I always obey lawful authority; and even unlawful, when I am opposed by a superior force; and, doubtless, you have a warrant for this proceeding, notwithstanding it appears a little extraordinary. I humbly think, (but there now, what business have I to think?) that you are not *now*, and upon this *occasion*, acting under your commission. The weakest however must go to the wall. Near twenty to one are great odds indeed at foot-ball. I surrender my citadel. You have taken us all prisoners. We march out; but leave the honours of war all your own. Your colours fly triumphant; and I hear the shouts of victory. We have

surren-

surrendered *at* discretion. It is a moot point, whether *to* discretion. But let us not wrangle about such little monosyllables. I certainly did yield to superiority of some kind or other; whether of discretion or force, let historians of the year one thousand seven hundred and ninety-three determine.

You have had your revenge;—let us now *parly*. You say, and we have it under your own hands, that you are gentlemen—you add indeed, *of this Theatre;* but, whether of this Theatre or not, a gentleman will behave like a gentleman in the Theatre, out of the Theatre, and all the world over:—So that I am sure I shall be heard with candour, now the first heat is a little subsided. Hang it, I wish you had put your own names to that puzzling paper of yours; I might then have said, Colonel O'Nokes, or Captain Stiles, or Lieutenant Doe, or Ensign Roe;—but now I can address you only by the awkward appellation, *Gentlemen of this Theatre.* Give me leave to omit that odd addition, and to say plainly, " Gentlemen"—as I have no doubt you are, by self-estimation, profession, and rank;— though in one instance, and from zeal in what you deemed your COUNTRY's CAUSE, you have acted rather *ungently* to be sure.

Gentlemen, then; we have mentioned the word *commiſſion*. You do not, I dare say, suppose, that military men only have *commiſſions*. Every clergyman has a *commiſſion*. Will you give me leave to read it to you? It may aſſiſt you in the judicial proceedings of this newly *united Court Martial and Court Eccleſiaſtical*. In the avocations of rural amuſement, and the fatigues of a military life, you may not perhaps have met with it, or conſidered it with due attention. Here it is, Gentlemen, in this little volume, whence my offenſive text was taken. Shall I read it *for* you, as you are rather diſconcerted by your recent exertion in the cauſe of your country? Then, pray take off your hats and your caps, and iſſue orders to the younkers in the rear to hold their babbling, and call no more hard names, now the parly has begun.—" Hats off?—what! to " *you?*—No; I'll be ——— if I do." Not ſo haſty, good Colonel O'Nokes, I did not ſay to *me*; but in reverence of the aforeſaid commiſſion, which comes from the KING—of
Kings.

Kings. The words are very solemn. Nothing should have induced me to have read them to you in this place, but that you have accused me in this place of having exceeded my commission in the offensive sermon, in which I studied to promote your happiness, and the happiness of every mortal under Heaven, by recommending, on gospel principles, peace and benevolence. Now your wrath is a little abated, and the overflow of ill language subsided, I will read it to you. In return, if you please, you shall shew me that part of your commission, which authorizes you to turn his Majesty's liege subjects out of Theatres, and to revile them as they go, with insulting language.

" *I charge thee, before* God, *and the* Lord
" Jesus Christ, *who shall judge the quick*
" *and the dead at his appearing, and in his*
" *kingdom,*

" *Preach the Word, be instant* in season,
" out of season, reprove, rebuke, ex-
" hort, *with all long-suffering and doctrine.*
" *For the time will come, when they will*
" *not endure sound doctrine, and shall turn*
" *away*

" *away their ears from the truth; but watch*
" *thou in all things; do the work of an Evan-*
" *gelist, make full proof of thy ministry.*"

St. Paul to Tim. ii. 4.

Now, Gentlemen, would you think one of your own profession deserving of abuse and insult for doing his duty, under all circumstances, fearlessly and regardless of interest and favour, according to the tenor of his *commission?* Would he be entitled to praise or blame? Do you despise a soldier who braves all danger, and esteem a sneaking coward who consults only his own safety? The questions are self-answered. Apply them, from your own profession, *mutatis mutandis*, to *another* profession, as liberal as your own; and still honoured, and deemed useful, even in a political light, to your COUNTRY, for which you display so much zeal. The Author of that religion, which is established by law in this kingdom, is called the CAPTAIN OF SALVATION. Would you have a soldier, professionally engaged in the service of this GREAT CAPTAIN, a mere time-server, a preferment hunter, a flatterer, a subtle politician for his own

own gain, a servile courtier, fit only to cringe and simper at levees, and bend his doctrines with his back to all circumstances and persons, for the sake of a stall or a mitre? Would you have him suit his doctrines from the pulpit to the varying hour, to the caprice, or the vanity, or the prejudice, or the passion of his congregation? Would you wish him to preach the reverse of my text, " Glory to
" *ourselves*, to great lords, generals, and worldly
" potentates *in the highest*; ON EARTH WAR;
" ill will *(for any thing we care)* to all men, but
" our friends, our relations, our patrons, and
" party?"—No; Gentlemen, you would not. I know you better than to believe it for one moment. Animated with the spirit of Englishmen, which loves a frank, honest disposition, you must prefer one who would preach what he thinks *useful truth*, even at the point of the bayonet, and the mouth of the cannon. Gentlemen, I wish I could claim the honour of such ardour in the service—All I can claim is, a desire to do my duty in the pulpit with fidelity. I preached peace in the hearing of those who, it now appears, were prejudiced, at the time, in favour of war. For that very

reason,

reason, it became me to do my duty with particular zeal:—I did it to the best of my power. I rejoice that I was enabled to do it so successfully, as to have excited their attention; even though it is accompanied with their displeasure. Prejudices obstruct the truth for a time; but they go off like clouds in an autumnal morning, when the sun rises in his glorious majesty. Eyes have some, but they will not see. Pride militates against persuasion. Pride says, " Who is it that speaks to *us* in a style " of authority?—Who is this that *dares* EX- " HORT us?"—Pride said formerly of our Saviour, " Is not this the carpenter's son?" Pride would have stoned him to death; and Pride did at last crucify him: But, when Pride had done its worst, the truths which a few proud men of his own time were offended at, TRIUMPHED OVER THE CIVILIZED WORLD;— the CROSS became the glory of nations, and princes, and warriors; and the proud were forgotten or execrated. I do not despair, even now, notwithstanding I was compelled to quit the Theatre, but, as the world improves in KNOWLEDGE, *war will be no more;* and, *perpetual and universal peace*, which I so earnestly contended for, will be at length established. In my generation, Gentlemen, I will do all I can to accelerate the approach of that happy period. I rejoice, greatly, that I preached peace at Brighton. It is my duty to preach it every where, when called upon to preach at all; and, by God's grace, I will do my duty. I thank you for your opposition; it will greatly promote the cause. On that account,

I am, Gentlemen,

Your much obliged

V. KNOX.

TUNBRIDGE-TOWN,
   KENT,
*Nov.* 29, 1793.

P. S. The next time you honour me with your correspondence, *venture*, if you wish for an answer, to sign your names to your epistle. It will be more manly than to sculk under that indefinite description of yourselves, " THE " GENTLEMEN OF THIS THEATRE."

# PREFACE

## TO THE

## PUBLIC.

*Sunt lachrymæ rerum et mentem mortalia tangunt.—*
*Projice tela manu.————* VIRG.

---

AT the ordination of every Prieſt, the following queſtion is put to him, in the moſt ſolemn manner, by the BISHOP:

"*Will you maintain and ſet forwards, as much as lieth in you,* QUIETNESS, PEACE, AND LOVE AMONG ALL CHRISTIAN PEOPLE, *and ſpecially among them that are, or ſhall be, committed to your charge?*"

To which the following is the anſwer:
" I WILL DO SO, *the Lord being my helper.*"

I conceive then it is the duty of every clergyman, bound by this promiſe, to preach PEACE

[ xx ]

ON EARTH and GOOD-WILL TOWARDS MEN, as well in a time of war as at any other time; as well to a congregation of Chriſtian people in the military profeſſion, as to a congregation of Chriſtian people in any other profeſſion.

In the intereſt of no party, the advocate of humanity\*, the friend of man, a lawfully ordained miniſter of Jeſus Chriſt, I have on all occaſions endeavoured to fulfil this ſolemn engagement, made at the time of ordination; and particularly in the laſt Autumn, when a large and mixed congregation, at a place of public reſort, was, on the morning of a Sunday

---

\* The following ſpecimens of HEATHEN ſedition, which I adopt, are pretty ſafe from informers, being, to *moſt* of *them*, in an unknown tongue:

" Homo ſum; humani nihil a me alienum puto."

TER.

" ——— Quis enim bonus, aut face dignus
" Arcanâ, qualem Cereris vult eſſe ſacerdos,
" Ulla aliena ſibi credat mala? Separat hoc nos
" A grege brutorum."

JUV.

" ——— Molliſſima corda
" Humano generi dare ſe natura fatetur,
" Quæ *lachrymas* dedit, hæc noſtri *pars optima* ſenſûs."

JUV.

in

in August, committed by the vicar to my charge.

The consequences of this endeavour are already known to many; but are circumstantially related in the following Narrative. I have long postponed, and now publish it with reluctance. The personal insult, unjustifiable as it was, should have been overlooked with *sovereign contempt*, as it deserved, if it had not been followed up by menaces and misrepresentation. A newspaper which is supposed to insert paragraphs under the sanction or with the connivance of *high authority*, expressed a hope that I should be told of my improper sermon " by my *diocesan, in a way* that would " make me an *example* to other PULPIT PO-" LITICIANS." Whether the example was to operate on courtly preachers of *fast sermons*, in favour of *war* and ILL-WILL TO MEN, I know not. Another paper informed the Public, that I was seeking safety by flight to America; but that I should probably be stopt in my course by the Attorney-General. Other prints, in the same service, generously undertook the task of throwing dirt upon an individual, in the hope that, where much was thrown,

thrown, some might stick; and that the *little irregularity* of the officers in desiring me " *to leave the Theatre,*" for so it is candidly expressed in a newspaper now before me, might be absorbed in the atrocity of my sermon. Private letters and conversation were equally kind to my *anonymous* assailants, and bitter against ME, whom they mentioned by *name*.

I therefore at first drew up the minutes of the whole transaction, for the information of my family,—a part of whom were involved in the affront intended for me alone. A time might come (after I should be gone to a juster Tribunal than the military one at the Theatre) when my younger children might ask what I had done to cause the men of violence to rise up against me, to excite the hope of *true Britons* that I should be punished by my diocesan, to urge me to meditate a retreat to America, and to occasion the projected voyage to be prevented by the interference of the Attorney-General. This *memorial* would have gratified their curiosity, and, I hope, removed their anxiety. I had preserved a record for their satisfaction; and I sat down, in the midst of the arrows that were thrown from unseen

unseen hands, perfectly contented. I had a MURUS AHENEUS to shelter me.

But my silence, which arose partly from contempt, and partly from a love of ease and peace, was misinterpreted. It was supposed, by the malignant, to imply a consciousness of having deserved the ill-treatment I had received. It was attributed to timidity. It was said to be the effect of a bribe. It was matter of astonishment to my friends, and exultation to my adversaries. The opportunity was seized for the dissemination of calumny. Malice, unmolested, stalked over the field in triumph. I was told, that the independent part of the Public expected an account authenticated by me; as they had been hitherto perplexed by recitals, apparently defective and clearly contradictory. I therefore determined to revise my notes; and I now present them to the Public, merely as the *record of a military outrage*, rendered important by their notice of it, by its mischievous tendency, and by its singularity.

Many years have I been in the habit of addressing my countrymen on the pleasant subjects

subjects of taste and literature; and they have listened to me with a degree of favour, which is the more entitled to my gratitude, in proportion as it has been too little deserved. My whole life has been devoted to the cultivation of letters; and the fruits, such as they were, have been consecrated to the public service. There are living witnesses to prove that my efforts originated in no *sordid motive*. I sought no gain, but the esteem of the Public. In this object I have not been entirely unsuccessful, if I may judge from the long-continued and widely-diffused circulation of my imperfect endeavours. I now at last, and for the first time, come before my fellow-citizens, in a cause in which I am *personally* concerned. I come not as a stranger to them. They have known me long, and they will indulge me with an impartial hearing, if it were only for my past honest, though feeble efforts in their service. I wish I were now to bring before them topics of general literature, or morals, or religion; such as have no connection with politics, or the bitterness of party spirit; but, in the wonderful vicissitudes of human affairs, it is my lot to appear as a culprit, accused by

*public*

*public report** of *sedition.* At the very sound of the charge, enemies unseen, unknown, unprovoked, are ready to overwhelm me if they dared, unheard, unprotected, undefended. Pains are taken to exasperate great and powerful bodies, even Government itself, against me. To whom can I have recourse but to the generous Public, against public misrepresentation? I am *compelled* to appeal to the people; because to them the misrepresentation has been made in daily newspapers. I appeal with confidence, supported by truth, a good cause, and a clear conscience.

In speaking of transactions in which I was principally concerned,

*Et quorum pars magna fui,*

I must of necessity speak in the *first person*, oftener than I approve; but egotism ceases to be a fault when it is unavoidable.

That I have always written freely, those who have done me the honour to read what I have written, will allow; and that I have

---

* It is the observation of an antient, that to credit *common report* is itself a species of calumny. CALUMNIÆ GENUS EST RUMORI CREDERE.

recommended earnestly, peace, order, subordination, liberty, and loyalty, they cannot deny.

To write and speak freely is the duty of every clergyman. His office demands and justifies it. It requires no apology, but deserves praise. That VERITAS ODIUM PARIT, or *truth makes a discourse* OFFENSIVE, is an old observation; but they who, regardless of their interest, voluntarily incur the odium which arises from doing their duty, are not culpable. A preacher ought to maintain the *freedom and dignity of the pulpit*, no less tenaciously than military men contend for the honour of arms. " *Pray for me,* " says St. Paul, *that utterance may be given* " *unto me, that I may open my mouth boldly,* " *to make known the mysteries of the gospel,* " *and that therein I may speak boldly,* as " I OUGHT TO SPEAK."

At Brighton church I did my duty, to the best of my power, with that boldness which the apostle approves, and which a good cause inspired. I retract not. I do not apologize. I rather thank God who gave me his grace to do my duty as I did; and I wish I had
been

been enabled to have done it more effectually. The sword should then have returned to its scabbard, there to rust; no longer a brilliant ornament, but an ugly incumbrance, viewed with horror. *They should no more hurt nor destroy in all the holy mountain.* Every man should *enjoy* the being God gave him; nor lose it, except for MURDER, until he who gave, should take it away. The fiercest beast of the forest, that prowls for prey, does not shed the blood of its own kind. Serpents bite not serpents. Lions kill not lions. The tiger preserves perpetual peace with the tiger. Bears live in concord with bears. But MAN puts the IRON, given him for the purposes of agriculture and mechanics, on the ANVIL, and manufactures it into a SWORD, and DECORATES AS A TOY, an instrument purposely designed for the destruction of his fellow MAN, and of no other use *.

In

---

\* ——" Serpentum major concordia; parcit
" Cognatis maculis similis fera ; quando leoni
" Fortior eripuit vitam leo? quo nemore unquam
" Expiravit aper majoris dentibus apri?
" Indica tigris agit rabidâ cum tigride PACEM
" PERPETUAM: sævis inter se convenit ursis.

" Ast

In the Proverbs of Solomon we read, that " THE FEAR OF MAN BRINGETH A SNARE:" a snare, which may entangle a man in time-serving, in adulation, in the cowardly concealment of necessary truth, through a dread of impeding or retarding his own preferment,

" Ast HOMINI FERRUM LETHALE incude nefandâ
" Produxisse parum est."        JUV. SAT. 15. Verf. 159.

Thus far a POOR HEATHEN; let a Christian preacher teach the same doctrine, and it becomes *wicked and seditious*, and renders him worthy of Botany Bay.

Horace is as wicked as Juvenal. I doubt whether both would not have been seditious enough to have refused to pray for success to fleets and armies, in the usual terms of *obsolete forms of prayer*, such as were used by our forefathers. Hear Horace.

" Quo quo, SCELESTI, ruitis? aut cur dexteris
    " A; tantur enfes conditi ?
" Neque hic LUPIS mos, neque fuit Leonibus
    " Unquam nisi in DISPAR genus."        HOR.

More Heathen treason: " *Nulla tam detestabilis pestis*
" *est, quæ non homini ab homine nascatur.*"        CIC.

" Cætera animantia in *suo* genere *probè* degunt; *congre-*
" *gari* videmus, et *stare* contra *dissimilia:* leonum feritas
" inter se non dimicat. Serpentum morsus non petit
" Serpentes, nec *maris* quidem belluæ nisi in diversa
" genera sæviunt. AT HERCULÈ HOMINI PLURIMA EX
" HOMINE SUNT MALA."        PLINII. PROEM. Lib. vii.

HOMO HOMINI LUPUS.

How the Christians make the Heathens blush!

or disturbing his own ease. I did not fall into this snare. In the cause of God, and of my fellow-creatures, I feared no man. Such a cause is a better breast-plate than triple brass; a more impregnable fortification than a *Vauban* or a *Lenox* ever invented.

What I said on war, was as applicable to the French, the Austrians, the Russians, the Prussians; to the Indians that SCALP, and to the Cannibals that EAT their enemies, as to any other people in the universe. Oh wretched degradation of human nature! In civilized and Christian countries, it is found necessary to hide the ugliness of war, (which goes naked among savages,) by pomp, finery, and GLORY. Ignorance is thus deluded. A great part of mankind are still GROSSLY ignorant, think little, and are fascinated with glitter. But silence the noise, and take off the tinsel and trapping, and the fascination is over. Divest Bellona's sword of its *pretty sword-knot* and its carved and gilt handle, and you blunt its edge. Change even certain *names*, and observe the effect. For war, read havoc; for conquest, read murder and devastation. Voltaire puts these words into the mouths of the

Quakers:

Quakers: " Our God, who has commanded us to love our enemies, and to suffer without repining, would certainly not permit us to cross the seas, merely because murderers clothed in scarlet, and wearing caps two feet high, enlist citizens by a noise made with two little sticks on a bit of dried asses skin. And when, after a victory is gained, the whole City of London is illuminated; when the sky is in a blaze with fire-works, and a noise is heard in the air of thanksgivings, of bells, of organs, and of cannon, we groan in silence, and are deeply affected with sadness of spirit, for the sad havoc which is the occasion of these public rejoicings." Now the Quakers are a plain people in their dress, but very *shrewd;* they are not caught by GLITTER, as larks by looking-glasses.

There are beings with two legs and unfeathered, (but not in Christian countries,) who appear as if they would care not, provided they could retain their titles and sinecures, if the whole human race had but one neck, and lay under the axe of the Guillotine. How happy we, who are blessed with the *Christian*

*tian religion*, and prove our SINCERITY as Chriſtians, by never entering on any wars, but when forced by *actual aggreſſion*. *Defenſive war* is certainly exempt from all the cenſure which falls on war wantonly and cruelly undertaken from pride and ambition. I always thought the *militia*, whoſe only buſineſs is defence, a moſt excellent inſtitution, and its officers, in general, men of true patriotiſm. May I take the liberty of quoting what I ſaid of them many years ago, in *Eſſays moral and literary?*

" I cannot cloſe this ſubject without applauding thoſe generous and liberal men, who, when their country was threatened with an INVASION, forſook all the comforts of their homes, and without previous habits to enure them, ſubmitted with alacrity to the inconveniences of a camp, and the unſettled life of a ſoldier. Their judicious and patriotic ardour evinces that they wear a ſword for their COUNTRY'S GOOD [*]."

I ſhall beg permiſſion to tranſcribe another paſſage, which has alſo been written many years, on the military in general.

[*] Eſſay 19, Edition thirteenth.

"Men in the military profession are not culpable for the existence of war; a state which they found established before they were born, and which it is not in their power, if it were their inclination, to alter. Their profession has always been deemed one of the most honourable. As things are constituted, and as they have generally conducted themselves, their claim to honour may, I believe, remain undisputed. While we lament that such an order of men should have been found necessary, we may freely bestow that praise, which the virtues of individuals engaged in it deserve.

"Courage is obviously a prime requisite in this profession. It has of course been cultivated, encouraged, and displayed by it in high perfection. But courage, when it does not arise from animal insensibility, is connected with every generous virtue. The soldier has, therefore, been distinguished for openness, honour, truth, and liberality. To the solid virtues, he has also added the high polish of urbane and easy manners. His various commerce with the busy world has rubbed off those asperities, and extended

" that narrowneſs, which too often adhere to
" the virtuous recluſe.  And perhaps it is
" difficult to exhibit human nature in a more
" amiable and honourable light, than it ap-
" pears in the accompliſhed ſoldier; in the
" ſoldier, fully prepared for his profeſſion by
" a liberal education, and finiſhed, through
" the favourable circumſtances of it, by all
" thoſe qualities which render men generous
" in principle, and agreeable in converſa-
" tion \*."

But though I am ready to honour, as I have ever publicly honoured, the military profeſſion; yet I wiſh, in the ſcripture-language, that " MEN MAY NOT LEARN WAR ANY MORE." But, ſays an objector, there always were wars.  It is granted.  But becauſe mankind have been unwiſe, are they never to relinquiſh their folly?  Why ſhould not human affairs, in this reſpect as well as others, admit of improvement, by THE TOTAL ABOLITION OF WAR?  Human affairs ſhould always be in a progreſſive ſtate.  The old age of the world,

\* Knox's Winter Evenings, page 295. octavo edition.

which

which is the present age, should correct the temerity of its youth; the enlightened state should rectify the errors of its past times of ignorance. Time was, when men did not believe the *existence of antipodes;* and when to have published an opinion of their existence, would have subjected the ingenious philosopher to the *inquisition;* and, perhaps, brought him to the *stake.* Time was, when men believed that the earth stood still, and that the sun and all the heavenly bodies rolled round it; and to have contradicted such an idea, would have been deemed damnable heresy. Time was, when people thought that Sir Isaac Newton's discoveries could never have been made. The time *still continues,* when men believe war to be necessary; though the very same men, at the same time, (in England at least,) allow, that the Christian religion is true, which forbids rancour, malice, revenge, and teaches forgiveness of INJURIES AND OF ENEMIES. The commandments are read in the churches of England by public authority; and one of them says, Thou shalt do no murder; yet a party shall surprize a few unarmed foreigners asleep in a village retreat, and put them

them to death if there is danger of their giving alarm, and expect, and even receive rewards and applause. The Bible, read also by law in our churches, contains this edict, founded in justice and mercy: "WHOSO "SHEDDETH MAN'S BLOOD, BY MAN ALSO "SHALL HIS BLOOD BE SHED;" yet, he who coolly sheddeth the blood of thousands, shall be received with acclamations, illuminations, bonfires, explosion of cannons; and be considered as worthy of the richest rewards and the highest honours a CHRISTIAN NATION can confer. Prejudice is very obstinate, and ignorance with great difficulty convinced. Yet I must believe, that a NEWTON may hereafter appear in the political world; and *prove* that men may live happily, the short space allowed them, without employing the *best part of their lives*, the time of youth, health, and strength, in cutting off each other from the land of the living. Is not the world wide enough for us all? We put PIKE, and other fishes of prey, into our fish-ponds, to eat up the little fish, that the others may fatten and become overgrown for the tables of the rich and luxurious: But it is quite another thing

[ xxxvi ]

among *Christians*, who are taught to say, "OUR
" FATHER which art in heaven;" and who,
consequently, are *all brethren*, and who cannot
slay any of their species, unless in self defence,
without being guilty of *fratricide*, an aggravated species of murder. "YE ARE BRETHREN,"
say the scriptures; " WHY DO YE WRONG
" ONE TO ANOTHER?"

GREAT GOD! the Father of us all, have
mercy on mankind, though their transgressions
have justly provoked thee, and grant, that
none of thy children may lead their brethren
to mutual destruction *. What, indeed, are
these leaders? Are they not shepherds of their
people †? Is it not the shepherd's business to
guard all the sheep from the common enemy,
the WOLF? Would a shepherd, a real, not a
figurative shepherd, be justified in leading one
flock to fight and destroy another, *even if they
would*, when thou hast given herbage sufficient for them all? But supposing, for argument's sake, *that shepherd himself one of*

---

\* Ολλυντας και ολλυμενους.
Πολλας δ'ιφθιμους ψυχας αιδι προιαψεν. HOM.

† Quid meruistis, oves? placidum pecus. OVID.

*the*

*the sleep*, would not his conduct, in teaching them to anticipate the butcher, be still more culpable, because more unnatural? But what are these leaders? Do they not enter the world in the same helpless manner as the poorest of their train? Do they not leave it, after a brief continuance, in the same helpless manner? and shall the short miserable interval be spent in destroying life, and diffusing misery? They themselves are objects of greater pity, than those who *innocently bleed* under their guidance. Have mercy upon them all, O Father! and grant that PRIDE AND AMBITION may FALL at last, subdued by reason, and by the influence of Christian benevolence. Let us all remember we are *men*, pity human nature, alleviate its woes, and retain but one cause of amicable strife, the EMULATION TO DO THE MOST GOOD IN OUR TIME, AND TO PREVENT THE MOST EVIL.

Happy they, who, in this turbulent scene, are enabled to live in peace, and descend to the grave unstained with the blood of any fellow-creature! Behold a pale hand in a shroud, spotted with the blood of a brother! not one penitential tear to wash it out! O earth, cover it! May neither my friends nor my enemies have to meet, in another world, those whom they have sent prematurely out of this, with all their imperfections on their heads. May they live in peace, die in charity, and be united in bliss, at a joyful resurrection. So much, surely, I may *wish* without the imputation of sedition.

With respect to the charge of sedition, I ask, I solicit the strictest scrutiny of my conduct, as a loyal citizen, as a preacher of peace, as a friend to order, law, and liberty. I hesitate not to add the word *liberty*, though *by some* \* proscribed. If I were not a friend to liberty,

---

\* To account for some late POLITICAL PHENOMENA, wonderful in a country whose CONSTITUTION IS FREE, and whose King was seated on the throne by the HAND OF LIBERTY, it may not be improper to consider the observation of an able writer; "There may be a "FACTION FOR THE CROWN AS WELL AS; "AND CONSPIRACIES AGAINST THE PEOPLE AS WELL AS "AGAINST PREROGATIVE."—"To form these ca-", says a remarker on this observation, "with small trouble, it "will be necessary to observe, that in every "society, a number of men to whom

liberty, as well as to law and order, I should indeed be a traitor; for liberty is the essence of the British Constitution.

To stifle useful truth by INTIMIDATION *, is an attempt as weak as it is wicked. It would

"requisite to RISE IN A FREE STATE. The emoluments
"and favours they gain for SUPPORTING TYRANNY, are
"the only means by which *they* can OBTAIN THOSE DI-
"STINCTIONS which, in every EQUAL GOVERNMENT, are
"the *rewards* of PUBLIC SERVICE."

\* The severity assumed by some parts of the community towards other parts of it, is thus accounted for, by that very able and respectable clergyman, the Rev. CHRISTOPHER WYVILL, whose exertions of eloquence and virtue, in the cause of freedom, deserve his country's gratitude.

"The establishment of a legislative assembly in France
"on equitable principles of representation; the exultation
"expressed by the people here, on the successful efforts
"which had been exerted to emancipate the French na-
"tion; and the apparent ease with which a transition
"might be made, in this country, from admiring their
"form of representation to *improving our own*; these
"united circumstances pushed the pride of a JEALOUS
"ARISTOCRACY to its present extremity.

"From that moment their ambition no longer has
"known any bounds of justice, decency, or even
"DECENCY.

"The

would be equally feasible to extinguish the light of the sun, by binding bandages over the eyes of men. Fire, sword, banishment, proscription, prosecution, strained even to persecution, have been often tried in attacking truth; but they have ultimately promoted the cause which they were intended to annihilate. Lop a tree, and, if the root is vigorous and the soil fertile, it will vegetate with redoubled luxuriance. It is one advantage, among a thousand, attending the conquests of reason, that they secure the regions which they subjugate. Brute force extends only to the body. The mind mocks its impotence. The FAULCHION, lifted up against PRINCIPLES, cuts the

" The PEOPLE, and their just constitutional claims, have
" been the constant objects of their UNQUALIFIED SCORN
" AND DERISION, their unmitigated ABHORRENCE AND EX-
" ECRATION; and still, in each wild and moody change of
" temper, these alternate EXCESSES OF RAGE and RIDI-
" CULE*, of HORROR and CONTEMPT, have been but the
" varied expressions of their FEAR."

*air*, which inftantaneoufly coalefces; while he who aimed the blow falls to the ground, by his own ill-directed force.

Nothing but a BELLUM INTERNECINUM, a war which cuts off man, woman, and child from the face of the earth, can exterminate falutary truth, once made vifible, by her own unextinguifhable luftre, to a whole people. The object cannot be deftroyed, though the eyes which fee it may be put out with the fword's point. Violence produces fear and death, but not conviction. It may fubdue, but cannot conciliate. Then *may violence ceafe from the earth*; and the mild arts of perfuafion, reafoning, and argument, be the *only* means reforted to, unlefs when it is neceffary to repel force by force, by all PEOPLE and RULERS in every part of the habitable globe. May the homage paid to grandeur be every where paid to virtue; the glory beftowed on warriors, referved for the peace-makers; and the laurel become lefs honourable than the olive.

In this age of viciffitude, under every change of political, philofophical, or religious opinion, be it mine, as far as in me lies, to promote peace, to diffufe happinefs, and to prevent

vent or alleviate misery. These are my party-principles—these my politics—this my philosophy—and this, with piety to GOD, and allegiance to the PRINCE OF PEACE, my RELIGION.

# A
# NARRATIVE
## OF
Transactions relative to a SERMON
Preached at *Brighton*, *August* 18, 1793.

---

THE contumelious language and insolent behaviour of a few angry persons, who thought proper to take offence at a Sermon which I lately preached at Brighton, have hitherto been passed over in silence, because I deemed them utterly unworthy my serious animadversion. As far as I was personally concerned, I despised them. I felt that superiority which arises from observing a silly effort of causeless malice, seeking its own poor gratification, by force, by the infringement of law, and the disturbance of order. Though injury was certainly intended me, yet, at the time, I suffered none; and I scorned either to complain of the attempt, or to retaliate the malevolence.

But the Public has confidered the outrage more ferioufly. To the Public it appears to afford an alarming precedent of military interference. It juftly excites general uneafinefs, when they who are bound by every obligation to preferve the peace, become its violators; and feek redrefs of fuppofed grievances, by arbitrary coercion, neglecting thofe laws which apply to every wrong a certain remedy. Nothing tends more directly to the ANARCHY we deplore. A military tribunal, to which even the pulpit is made amenable by force, is indeed a fingular and truly alarming innovation in our excellent Conftitution. The Public is naturally rouzed at the flighteft appearance of military defpotifm, the worft of all others; and of that *unauthorized* violence, which has produced, in its progrefs, the moft dreadful maffacres on the other fide of the Channel. To the Public, thus awakened by a dangerous example, I owe a faithful and minute Narrative of all the circumftances which have excited its folicitude.

The

The public attention calls loudly for my statement. Misrepresentation and calumny have taken advantage of my forbearance. The engines of venal malice have been employed, to hurl on me their envenomed weapons of abuse. Diurnal papers, notoriously under corrupt influence, have been commissioned to misrepresent my sermon and my principles, that the offence of those who endeavoured to punish me in a manner equally illegal and indecorous, might be supposed to admit of palliation. An unoffending individual was to be sacrificed, that a nameless body of his favoured assailants might escape censure. I owe to my friends and to myself a public representation of the whole affair, to obviate the effects of base calumny, which, though despicable in the eyes of those who know its origin, is yet diffused with industry, enforced by influence, and at length deceives the unwary.

I beg not to be misunderstood in the motives to this publication. I mean not to complain. I seek no redress; for I feel no evil. The feeble weapon aimed at me fell pointless to the ground, and I smiled at its imbecillity.

I wish only to leave on record a true account of a transaction, which, insignificant to myself at first, has derived importance from the continued attention of the Public to it, and from the indefatigable calumnies of agents, who, for the purposes of their paymasters, are mercenary enough to palliate any wrong done to a private individual.

I am sensible that a preacher of the gospel of Jesus Christ, when he has performed his duty in the pulpit to the best of his power, and according to the dictates of his conscience, ought to bear with patience whatever ill usage may ensue. I know well, that he ought to practise, what he is bound to preach, the forgiveness of injuries. I am aware that he ought to stifle the feelings of resentment, and to return good for evil. But I am also convinced, that it is his duty to stop the progress of error, and to do himself and others justice, by a representation of real facts, neither distorted nor discoloured by guile.

It has indeed been my lot to have suffered ill-treatment from those who were bound by all the laws of honour to have afforded me, and those who accompanied me, protection from UNMANLY infult. *The age of chivalry is paſt;* or the ladies of my family would not have participated in the puniſhment to which I was condemned, as an *eccleſiaſtic*, by a *military* ſentence. Though I could not but feel ſome degree of indignation at thoſe circumſtances of the inſult which involved defenceleſs females in it; yet I have endeavoured to ſubdue all emotions of revenge. I purpoſely abſtained from animadverting on the affront intended me, till time co-operating with reaſon, ſhould have effaced the firſt impreſſions, and ſoftened anger into pity. I am diveſted of all vindictive ſentiment, and proceed with perfect equanimity to my Narrative.

At the commencement of an anniverſary vacation in the laſt Autumn, I hired a houſe in North Street, Brighton, and went thither, together with my family, in purſuit of health, by ſea-bathing, and a ſalutary change of air and ſcene. A cloſe attention to ſtudy, and to various buſineſs, had rendered ſuch excurſions, in ſeaſons of leiſure, highly uſeful, if not neceſſary. In this temporary reſidence at a place of public reſort, I had no other object in view

but

but health. After I had been there a week or ten days, Mr. HUDSON, the vicar of the parish, with whom I had not then the pleasure of being in the least acquainted, sent me a note, expressing his desire that I would *gratify* his congregation, as he politely expressed himself, with a sermon on the morrow, which was Sunday the eleventh of August. I use his words, and appeal to him for the truth of the fact, it having been asserted in letters, in private companies, and at coffee-houses, that I solicited an opportunity to preach, in order to serve the purposes of a party. Short as the notice was, I did not refuse, especially as upon my shewing reluctance, some friends who were present at the receipt of the request, importuned me to comply.

On the Sunday I preached on the text, " *The peace of God, which passeth all under-* " *standing, shall keep your hearts and minds* " *through Christ Jesus.*"— Philipp. iv. 7.

As it has been said that I obtruded myself into the pulpit, and as I have been so singularly insulted and so grosly abused in public, I may be pardoned in mentioning in public, the

very

very flattering manner in which this sermon was heard by a very large and very respectable congregation, in which were many of the military belonging to the Surrey regiment, quartered in Brighton. The utmost attention was paid to it. The military appeared to be particularly impressed, and highly satisfied. Expressions of approbation were heard, too emphatic for me to repeat. Mr. HUDSON, the vicar, who read prayers, came to my house, on purpose to thank me, in his own name, and that of his congregation. He mentioned the general satisfaction I had given; the many inquiries that had been made after my name by strangers; and expressed a hope, that I would preach once more, as he knew it was the wish of his parishioners. This, however, I declined at that time, and certainly had no intention to preach again at Brighton, though I had every reason to be pleased with my reception.

I hope I may be permitted to mention a few additional circumstances, tending to evince that it was the wish, not only of the vicar and parishioners, but of the company resorting to Brighton, that I should preach there

there again. On my going to the usual places of public resort, gentlemen highly respectable in appearance, whom I had never spoken to before, paid me the compliment of noticing me by salutation; and several of them introduced themselves to me on the Stene, and at the bookseller's, in order to thank me for my sermon. One gentleman in particular, who told me his name is FOSTER, and who lives in Warwickshire, a perfect stranger, did me the honour to compliment me in a very remarkable manner, and to spend much time with me in various conversation. I have never seen him since I left Brighton, nor have had any communication with him; but I doubt not that he will do me the justice to acknowledge that he expressed the highest approbation, and added, that he had heard many do the same. I met upon the Stene, on the Monday morning, Captain MITFORD of Upper Charlotte Street, London, who told me that he had heard with great pleasure the singular applause bestowed on my sermon preached the day before, and lamented his own absence. These gentlemen, of whose integrity I have the highest opinion, will bear ample testimony to the

truth

truth of this part of my statement, and prove that I did not preach at Brighton against the will of the hearers, as malicious reporters have falsely, yet confidently, asserted.

I must regret, as circumstances have happened, that I did not make myself acquainted with the names of all the strangers, who honoured me with particular notice, in consequence of my sermon. They would all have confirmed my contradiction of a malicious report, that my *first* sermon at Brighton gave offence, and that I preached a second time officiously, against the wishes of the vicar and people, and at my own solicitation. To the vicar, and to the numerous inhabitants of Brighton, I make my appeal with confidence.

I proceed to mention how it happened that I was persuaded to preach on the following Sunday, after having declined it. On the birth-day of the PRINCE OF WALES, I was present at the ball, and partook of the supper given at the Castle in honour of him. I there also experienced a marked civility, from persons who could know me only from the sermon which had been so favourably received on the Sunday. I met Mr. HUDSON there.

He shewed great kindness, continued in my company nearly the whole of the evening, and in the course of it, renewed his request, that as his parishioners very much wished it, I would give him another sermon on the following Sunday. My reply was as follows: " I come here for recreation, after the fatigues of my daily avocations and of my own parish church, and I do not wish to be interrupted by exertions of this kind, especially as I find my last sermon has excited so general an attention, and probably raised expectation too high. You mention the praises I have received; but I will not preach for the sake of praise. If you say it will serve you, if you wish to be absent, or if it is any relief to you, I will endeavour to prepare a sermon in the midst of the interruptions of this place, and will preach next Sunday, though I sincerely wish to decline it." He continued his request, and I complied; little thinking how great a disturbance was to be the result.

I had no sermon with me which was suited entirely to the occasion. I had frequent visitors at my house, and was engaged to go out on family-parties for several days. However, I wrote the *offensive* sermon in short intervals, frequently interrupted. My enemies have said that I came prepared to Brighton, a missionary of sedition, an incendiary with my ammunition in my pocket, a preacher of premeditated treason, an emissary employed to cause mutiny in the army, and revolution in the empire. Such malice can only provoke a smile. Several friends saw me writing my sermon, and many can attest on oath, that I never sought an occasion of preaching at all at Brighton, as well as that I never preached sedition, treason, or any thing but what was at once conducive to public order and peace, and to private happiness, comfort, and security.

I chose for my subject, "*The prospect of perpetual and universal peace to be established on the principles of Christian philanthropy.*" My text was, *Glory to God in the highest, on earth peace, good-will towards men.*

I was led to the choice of this subject from observing the EXTREME BITTERNESS expressed, even in gay and good-humoured companies, against a great part of our fellow-creatures; from the almost daily accounts I the newspapers of slaughtered thousands, and the eagerness with which war had been adopted by all the nations concerned, when NEGOTIATION might have effected every desirable purpose, without expence, and without CARNAGE.

The following expressions, which were uttered loudly in my hearing, and apparently intended for my ear, on the Sunday evening on the Stene, after my second sermon, seem to prove that a recommendation of *good-will towards men* was not ill-timed. "My prayer," said an unknown gentleman in uniform, " my prayer to God is, that the war with France may be a long, a bloody—nay, an everlasting war." A similar INVETERACY I had often observed in conversation of mixed companies; and I had read something approaching to it, in *fast sermons* of recent date. I really thought, therefore, that a spirit so unphilosophical, so unchristian, so inhuman, ought to be checked, if possible, in the pulpit, by those who were enlisted soldiers under the PRINCE OF PEACE. The temper of the people seemed to be soured by national animosity, artfully inspired by delusive publications; and a sa-

*vageness*

vageness of sentiment began to prevail, productive of barbarism and barbarity. Persons wholly ignorant of public affairs, and incapable of judging of them, had been taught of late to express themselves with a CRUELTY against the public enemy, disgraceful to the British character, and such as, if farther encouraged by inflammatory treatises, may produce a conduct at home, in future circumstances, fatal to internal peace and personal safety. It must ever be dangerous to cherish CRUEL passions in the populace. He is a wretched politician, who, for temporary purposes, encourages sentiments in the common people inconsistent with their religion, and with humanity. Such being my opinion, I was confident I could not render greater service, in the little space allotted to a discourse from the pulpit, than in preaching universal philanthropy, and the duty of seeking peace with all human kind, by every possible mode of fair negotiation. These were the reasons which induced me to chuse the subject of *peace and good-will towards men.* The time and the place naturally suggested the idea. Such subjects, I am sure, are proper at all times,

times, and in all places; but there appeared to me a peculiar propriety in bringing them forward at the time I was defired to preach, and at Brighton. It was a time, when every news-paper teemed with accounts of dreadful flaughter. It was a place, at which the fubject of peace and war was peculiarly interefting, becaufe an army of many thoufand men was encamped in its vicinity, and the whole neighbouring country had affumed a warlike appearance. The church is a place at all times adapted to the doctrines of peace and benevolence. Had I even gone to the camp, and difcourfed, as a *chaplain*, on the fame topic, it could not have been out of place. But every one who came to the *church*, knew that he *muft* hear peace, charity, good-will, forgivenefs of enemies recommended, in hearing the leffons from the gofpel. If my fermon was deemed ill-placed in recommending univerfal peace and univerfal good-will in Brighton *church*, what will men, who judge fo, fay of the gofpel read there? what of the national liturgy, eftablifhed by law as firmly as the national militia?

But I digrefs too long from my Narrative.

On

On the Sunday appointed, I went, accompanied by a friend and all my family, to the church, and preached that sermon which gave displeasure to a *very few military men*, who, I am willing to believe, totally misapprehended its tendency. I was heard in silence, and, if I can judge, with great attention. I was not conscious that any part of the congregation was offended, nor did I surmise it till after the following incident. On going out of the church, a lady, a perfect stranger, accosted me and said, " I thank you for your sermon. I could have sat hours to have heard such with pleasure. But excuse me—I must tell you, that from what I have observed in the pews, among a certain description of persons, you have offended those, who, I fear, have as little relish for the doctrine of forgiveness as they seem to have of peace. Many, like myself, are highly pleased with every part of your discourse; but there are those who are angry indeed!" My family, who stood around me, heard her observations, and were greatly alarmed. I was not in the least *alarmed*, though certainly concerned, to find that I had been misapprehended. Conscious

scious of having meant nothing but what was humane, beneficent, and truly Christian, in all which I had delivered, I feared no ill. Having done no wrong, nor intended any thing but good, I felt a serene complacency, notwithstanding the alarm given by this unknown lady, in a tone of voice, and with a look and manner expressive of apprehensions for my safety. I met with no molestation in the church. I walked slowly through the church-yard. Nothing but respect was shown me. I returned with my family to my house with peculiar cheerfulness, flowing from a faithful discharge of my duty, and the consequent esteem of the parishioners, which, I believe, I possessed.

I had friends to dine with me on that day, and the church-service in the afternoon began rather early. Under these circumstances I might have been absent without blame. But I rose from my table, acquainting my company, that as I understood the officers, who were at church in the morning, were offended at me, I would certainly *walk* to church, in the hope of meeting some of them, and hearing what had given them offence, and of

coming

coming immediately, before misrepresentation could take place, to a full and amicable explanation. I wished earnestly to meet the angry parties, that we might converse together, that I might acknowledge my fault, if I had been in the wrong, and remove their mistake if they thought *me* so, undeservedly. I had no resentments; I only wished for reconciliation. I went therefore unaccompanied by my friends; for I sought no protection: I met not a single officer. After hearing Mr. Mossop preach, I returned to my family to drink tea. In the evening I proposed walking on the Stene, still hoping to meet my offended hearers in the military profession: many officers were there, but I did not recognize any of those who were at the church.— No insult was offered me; for I can hardly suppose that the speech above-mentioned, expressing a wish for a long, a bloody, nay an everlasting war, could be intended as an insult to *me*, though it was repeated close to my ear, in a voice raised above the common pitch, and with peculiar emphasis. My sermon was talked of frequently in my hearing, but not with disapprobation. I was pointed out as the preacher rather particularly indeed, but not rudely.

rudely. I perceived a large party of the military affembled at the caftle, who were dining in a room which looked immediately on the Stene; and I paffed them unavoidably. I met with no infult on this public and crowded walk, though I purpofely remained there till it was dark, and all the company began to retire. The inhabitants of Brighton, and the parifhioners in general, behaved with their ufual civility; not the leaft degree of rudenefs did I on this occafion, or at any time, experience from them, or from any of the company reforting to that place, unconnected with the offended FEW, in the military line.

On my return home, a letter was brought to me, of which the following is a copy:

" A ftranger prefents his compliments and
" fincere homage of thanks to Dr. *Knox*, for
" his moft excellent Sermon preached this
" morning, and earneftly requefts him to
" publifh it, as a means to promote the in-
" terefts of humanity, and procure that great
" defideratum, " Peace on Earth."

" The ardour of Chriftian philanthropy it
" breathes fhould be diffufed throughout the
" world, which is the object of this applica-
" tion.

" tion. The writer wishes to distribute a
" number of copies in a distant county. A
" dissemination of such enlightening and
" convincing knowledge is only wanting to
" stop the effusion of human blood; for
" when mankind are well awakened, they
" will not permit the dignified human but-
" chers, the insolent, unfeeling traffickers in
" blood, to lead them to destruction.

" *Sunday, Aug.* 18."

This anonymous letter, the honest effusion of philanthropy, I insert in this place, as it forms a part of my narrative. I have no suspicion whence it came. The servant, who delivered it at the door, went away in great haste. Several friends were present when the letter came, and read it as soon as it was opened.

I beg leave to mention in this place, that from the pulpit, where I must have had a pretty good view of the whole church, I saw very few officers; and of those few, I knew not one even by name: I thought there were not a dozen. Of common soldiers the number was also inconsiderable; I think there were

were scarcely twenty, and these were not of the camp, but of the Surry militia quartered in the town. There were indeed more of the same regiment in the porch or in the church-yard; but too remote from the pulpit to hear a syllable of sedition, if there had been any to hear. I mention the paucity of officers and privates for the following reason: the Public has been taught by mistaken prints to believe, that I was guilty of preaching peace and good-will before the *whole camp*, that the aisle was crowded with soldiers, and that all the officers of the camp attended. I appeal to the parishioners present, whether the number of military men, privates and officers included, was greater than I have conjectured. My sermon was not exclusively calculated for a congregation of persons in any particular profession. There was not a word addressed by an *apostrophe*, as I have heard it asserted, to the officers. I had no reason to suppose that any military men, but those of the Surry militia quartered at Brighton, would be at the church. I thought, and I believe it was so, that divine service was performed by the chaplains in the camp, and that the *officers of the camp*

*camp* would not be permitted to ftraggle to the town or the church, on a Sunday, during divine fervice. The Public has been much deceived in the exaggerated accounts of my preaching to the *whole army;* but had the whole army been at the church, had it been allowed or been poffible, I am certain they would have heard nothing from me, but what was authorized by the gofpel, enforced by the law of men as well as of God, tending to promote their happinefs in all events, and animating them to the difcharge of every duty, on principles of humanity and Chriftianity. I exprefsly afferted, while I was deploring the calamities of war, that the conductors of war were often men of SINGULAR HUMANITY AND HONOUR. I exprefsly commended the beautiful gradation of ranks in fociety. I enforced good order; I deprecated anarchy as much as defpotifm.

I have already related the tranfactions of the Sunday. On Monday I went to the Downs, where the whole army was affembled. The beauty of the day attracted thither my friend, and my family. I hoped alfo to meet thofe whom I had offended,

that

that they might bring their charge againſt me face to face; and that I might explain what was miſunderſtood, or make a frank acknowledgment, if any thing could be made appear on my part truly reprehenſible. I hoped the explanation on both ſides would be liberal, candid, and gentlemanlike. I cared not how many were preſent at it. Truth loves the light. I would not be protected by my company, or concealed in my carriage. I walked alone a great part of near four hours on the ground, amidſt thouſands; the reſt I ſpent with my viſitor, with my family, and the family of my friend, Mr. BRIDGER of Buckingham-houſe, Shoreham. The military were indeed engaged in their evolutions; but they frequently paſſed me nearly, and might have ſpoken to me. The company of ſpectators was very numerous, and much of it connected with the army. My ſermon, I have been ſince told, was a frequent topic of converſation on the ground, and I was pointed out as the preacher of it; but no inſult was offered, and no perſonal application made to me. In the evening I went, as uſual, to the Stene, and the bookſellers ſhops on the Stene, and

and met with nothing in either place, though crowded, but friendſhip and civility.

The morning of Tueſday was ſpent on the Stene, and in other places near Brighton. Even now I avoided not meeting thoſe who, I had been recently told, were heard to *threaten* me ſeverely, behind my back, on the preceding day. I preferred meeting them, and hearing the worſt they could ſay, to SECRET CALUMNY; which, as it could not be encountered, could not be repelled. This fiend was buſily at work, inflaming many againſt me who had never ſeen or heard me. Every one knows how things are unintentionally exaggerated when they become topics of converſation in the convivial hour, and when an emulation prevails of making a diſplay of ſpirit or ingenuity. Saucer-eyed phantoms of Sedition began to flit before diſturbed imaginations. Old women, dreaming of *chimeras dire*, ſtimulated their huſbands to buckle on the helmet and the ſhield, and take the ſpear, and go forth againſt the giant Sedition, which appeared to their old eyes in the form of a windmill.

The important hour at length approached. The anger of my enemies was nothing indeed

in

in duration to the wrath of Achilles; but yet it appears to have been of a durable nature. The offence of Sunday morning was to be revenged on Tuesday evening. My friend, who was to return to London on the next day, proposed that some of my family and myself should accompany him to the Theatre. I had no desire to go; but as I had determined to decline no opportunity of meeting those who, now, it seems, expressed themselves with great RANCOUR against me, I consented immediately. Accordingly Mrs. Knox, my eldest son (a boy of fourteen years), and my daughter (a year or two younger), set out with my friend for the Theatre. As we walked up North-street, several persons stopped and spoke to each other, in the hearing of myself and family, in terms of the highest approbation of the last Sunday's sermon. Near the door of the Theatre, MAJOR TORAINE and a young Lieutenant of the East Middlesex overtook me: they were not going to the Theatre; but they accompanied me a little way, and behaved with great politeness; the Major inviting me to visit him in the camp, and expressing his concern that he had not seen me there before. They might not perhaps

have

have heard of my offence; but, whether they had or not, it is certain that their behaviour was, as usual, friendly and gentleman-like. I have been since informed by a gentleman, who had opportunities of conversing in the camp, that, notwithstanding the misrepresentations of my sermon, a great part of the most respectable officers were far from expressing displeasure at its doctrine.

On entering the Theatre, Mr. Thomas, the boxkeeper, accosted me by name, though I thought I was unknown to him; shewed uncommon attention, and begged leave to seat us all in a good place of his own choice. This place was the right hand side-box, next to the stage-box.

Soon after the curtain drew up, a few officers entered the stage-box on the opposite side of the Theatre. They had not been there five minutes, before their whole attention seemed fixed on the box where my family, my friend, and myself were seated. They looked frequently at me, and then talked to each other with great apparent earnestness. Other officers, and several elderly ladies, soon appeared in the same box; they also looked at us in a

pointed

pointed manner, and then seemed to deliberate\*. Their attention appeared to be engrossed by the consultation, and they seldom turned to the players on the stage. There were several other officers interspersed in other boxes. Messages were sent to some of them, and they removed into the stage-box. A man who sat in the same box, and on the same seat with me, was sent for, and I saw him taking his seat opposite to me. They frequently went to each other, and appeared extremely busy and anxious in concerting the plan of operations. This continued during the whole of the play. My children observed it, and told me that they suspected some insult. I disregarded their suggestions, and sat with perfect composure. Between the play and the entertainment, the following Note, directed to me, was first handed from behind us, to Mrs. Knox, who gave it to me. My son had seen one of the officers writing; and there is no doubt but he was composing this Note, sent without a name, and couched in terms of caution and subtlety. I must call it a *discreet Note;* and as discretion is allowed to be the better part of courage, I must add

---

\* Aliquid jamdudum invadere *magnum!*     Virg.

another

another epithet, and contend that it is a courageous Note.

*Copy of the* MANDATE *of Expulsion, dispatched by a Confederacy of unknown Persons, styling themselves in the said Mandate,* THE GENTLEMEN OF THIS THEATRE. *Superscribed on the back,* Dr. KNOX.

" YOUR DISCOURSE LAST SUNDAY WAS
" SO OFFENSIVE, THAT THE GENTLE-
" MEN OF THIS THEATRE DESIRE YOU
" WILL QUIT IT IMMEDIATELY."

It is so laconic that it might be taken for the production of a Spartan Republican, if it were not at the same time so authoritative as to resemble the edict of a German Despot. It is written with a pencil on a scrap of torn paper. I intend to preserve it, that it may supply documents to future historians, and hope to have interest enough to get it deposited in the archives of the Tower.

I read the order, and gave it to Mrs. Knox. Immediately I rose, and addressing myself to the opposite boxes, which, however, were now nearly empty, *the military having accompanied their dispatch,* requested to know who

who had sent me this impertinent Paper without a name. The messenger, whoever he was, had disappeared. I turned back to look for him, and beheld a phalanx of military men, who had come round, and were drawn up behind me at the door of my box, and in the Lobby, through which I must pass in my retreat. While I was asking for the messenger, a clamour began, and finding the passage closed by the very persons who had ordered me to withdraw *immediately*, I stept a little forward, and endeavoured to say to the Theatre, which was not half filled, " Ladies
" and gentlemen, I have this moment received
" an extraordinary Paper, neither signed nor
" dated, containing a requisition that I should
" quit the Theatre immediately, on account of
" the sermon which I preached last Sunday
" morning in your parish church. I beg par-
" don for interrupting you, but under these
" circumstances, and surrounded, as you see
" I am, I humbly intreat the permission of
" the House, to ask aloud who sent me this
" Note, and by what authority I am bound to
" obey it, in this place of public entertainment,
" when my family and myself have entitled
" ourselves

" ourselves to unmolested seats, by paying the
" price demanded at the door. We have inter-
" rupted nobody. Will you authorize the ar-
" bitrary expulsion of us all? for my family and
" friend will certainly follow me. I beg leave,
" besieged as you see me by a considerable
" number of men behind me, who are at this
" moment expressing their anger by opprobri-
" ous names, to enter into a short explanation
" with them, to ask the particulars of my
" offence in *your presence*, and to declare, that
" if any thing advanced in my sermon gave
" personal offence, it was unintentional, and
" that I am concerned at it. If any of these
" gentlemen will prove to your satisfaction that
" he is justly offended, I will immediately beg
" his pardon. I beg *your* pardon, who are to-
" tally unconcerned in this attack, for this sin-
" gular interruption, which I trust I shall ob-
" tain from you, as men and Englishmen;
" when you have before your eyes a defenceless
" individual, in a situation so singular, as will,
" I hope, justify my present address to you."

It was impossible to be heard distinctly. I could not find an interval of silence to utter half of the above, which I had conceived in my my mind and wished to deliver. The clamour of the persons in uniforms behind me was loud and incessant. I heard myself called, in the first instance, a *democratical scoundrel that deserved to be hanged.* " A " Democrat, a Democrat, a d——d Democrat. " Out with the Democrat—no Democrats." Scoundrel and rascal were titles lavishly bestowed. It is needless to repeat the silly oaths and unmeaning expletives which served those, who were too much enraged to be able to say any thing else, to add to the noise and drown my voice. I particularly remember hearing one man say, " No speech—that " won't do—he ought to be hanged—out with " him :" and another call repeatedly for PERSONAL VIOLENCE to be inflicted upon me before I should be suffered to depart. A grim and gaunt figure exclaimed, " IRONS—IRONS, " here; he ought to be put in IRONS directly."

I found it was impossible to be heard by the House at large, who could not know the cause of the disturbance. I thought my perseverance might create a riot. I said, therefore, to my terrified family, " I will go, " for the sake of peace. Fear not, they will
" not

" not hurt WOMEN AND CHILDREN I feel
" no anxiety for my own safety. There is no
" opposing so great a superiority of num-
" bers. I hope for an explanation."

I entered the Lobby, and had a right to expect that the *passage would be clear*, and that I should be allowed to retire, as I was ordered, without molestation. But I found the narrow Lobby crowded by persons in regimentals, many of whom, as I passed, continued to use the same language which I had heard behind me, while in the House. No one, however, offered any *personal violence*, though ONE fellow, not *in an uniform*, (to the honour of the army,) continued to call loudly and repeatedly for it. He did not think proper to approach me; for what reasons I know not. Probably for prudential ones; and discretion, it has already been observed, is a valuable ingredient in the composition of valour. He was vox *et preterea* NIL. He did not begin to bray, till the whole body of veterans stood around him. Conscious safety fired his TONGUE.

When I had arrived—*per tot discrimina rerum*—at the opposite side of the House, I entered a box, and again attempted to speak to the very few quiet people in the Theatre, who conftituted the whole of the audience, except my purfuers, and were, I think, friendly. They knew little of what was paffing in the Lobby. They perhaps furmifed that fome French emiffary or fpy had been difcovered, and was taken into lawful cuftody by the *defenders of our country*. I addreffed them, and they would have heard me with attention. A few of them recognized me, and cried *Silence*; but the noife of my affailants continued. It was infifted that I fhould not fpeak to the people. " Go," faid one who came up to me *much out of breath*, " go directly—" go you muft:" while from behind refounded the cry, " Out with him—a Democrat, a " Democrat, a Democrat—*da capo*—a Demo-" crat.—No Democrat, a d——d Democrat." I wonder, in their patriotic zeal, they did not exclaim, *No people! no people! no people for ever.*

I now began to withdraw from the houfe; for the Poet fays,

——*Parere neceffe eft—*
*Nam quid agas? cum te furiofus cogat, et idem*
" ARMATUS."

But

But I was determined, at all events, to find Mrs. Knox and the children, who had been separated from me in the Lobby. On turning back, I saw Mrs. Knox in tears very near me, but without my daughter, and in great distress. I then requested, and insisted, that I might be permitted by the rushing phalanx to attend Mrs. Knox, and fetch both my son and daughter. While I was contending for this indulgence, and received no other answer than, " Go—go directly—go you must and " shall, by God," my family and friend came up to me. The generous victors shewed clemency at last, and suffered us, children and all, on our surrender, to march out unmolested. It is said, they returned immediately to their post in the stage-box; and that *loyal tunes* were played by the band in celebration of the triumph, by way of *Te Deum*, or, " *The horse* " *is thrown and his rider*," or some similar EPINIKION, sung while Princes were dragged at their chariot-wheels, in honour of the rivals of my assailants, the conquerors of antiquity.

On inquiring of Mrs. Knox what passed in the Lobby, while she and the children were separated from me, she informed me, that a

tall

tall officer, on her turning back to see for her daughter, pushed her violently by the shoulder, and bid her go *along after her husband and be d———d.* Another, who probably saw and was ashamed of this behaviour, and to whom I am really obliged for this tenderness, small as it was, to a woman in her situation, did say to Mrs. Knox, " No per-" sonal violence shall be used; he should not " have come among us." Another, nodding his terrific plumes, exclaimed, " It is well his " wife and children are with him, or else—" here he used a fine *aposiopesis*. A student in rhetoric might indeed, on this occasion, have learned the use of many fine figures of speech; but he may succeed equally well in the antient and celebrated school of Billingsgate. Mrs. Knox, who was really anxious for my safety, not having perhaps remarked that barking dogs do not always bite, used all her eloquence in expostulation, and in supplicating by the silent language of tears for clemency. But she was *hurried* along, and her gown and other parts of her dress *accidentally* torn in pieces. She has preserved them as TROPHIES in their lacerated state. Thus the only *personal violence* 

(which

(which the *Knight of the terrible tongue* called for) was exercised on a defenceless female, weeping for her husband, and intreating to be permitted to return and conduct her daughter in safety, who had been forced in the crowd from the protection of both father and mother. Temporary rage got the better, not only of military politeness, and the unmeaning forms of decorum, but of common humanity *.

My son, who was also separated from us in the Lobby, informed me that he ventured to say loudly, in an honest zeal for his father, " What are you doing? is this fair? so many " against one! Fie upon you!—near twenty " against one, O for shame!" Upon this a tall officer, whether the same who assaulted his mother or not he does not know, shook him violently, saying at the same time, " Who " are you, you dog? you ought to be hanged, " as well as your father, if it is your father; " and all such as hold his democratical prin- " ciples, you dog you!"

To my *very young daughter*, who was left behind us all; who, from a peculiar

* Vich amor Patriae, laudumque immensa Cupido.

Virg.

tender,

tenderness of disposition, was particularly distressed, and whom my friend was leading along with great difficulty, no other consolation was offered by MEN, who probably were themselves FATHERS, than a rough address, "Don't fret—what do you fret for?"—A little kindness to my daughter in such distress, would have taught me to forget my own ill-usage in my gratitude. But we were a family of *Democrats*, I suppose; and it was PURE PATRIOTISM that taught the defenders of our peace and liberties to treat us ALL with indiscriminate indignity, to forget, in their COUNTRY's cause, what was due to themselves, due to me and mine, and due to PUBLIC ORDER.

The world has been told, that they were a parcel of *drunken* boys who committed this outrage. There were some young men among them; but the RING-LEADERS, and the abettors, were, if I may judge from appearance, *veterans* in age if not in service, and of some rank, if I may believe report, in their perdition. They did it in SOBER sadness.

One circumstance I must beg leave to point out as particularly worthy of notice.—Of the assailants in the Theatre, *very few* (I believe)

lieve) were my *hearers in the church:* so that the rest were probably influenced by the false representations of gossips, and the dreams of old ladies, to which I have above attributed some of the ill-grounded alarm and offence. Whether any thing which they *thought* glanced at the *finery* of their old beaux, hurt the pride of the elderly gentlewomen, I cannot ascertain: but their instigations seemed to have considerable effect in stimulating the *corps*, who came into action *in the straits of the Lobby*, to the most valorous exertion.

After the defeat, our little family party walked home arm in arm, with our good friend, to our house in North-street. In the terrified condition of the ladies, a carriage and the attendance of a servant were desirable; but we were not suffered to wait for them. None of those polite gentlemen expressed any concern, lest the ladies, heated by the crowd in the Lobby, should catch cold; or offered to send for our accommodations from home. True politeness, that politeness which arises from a polished understanding and an humane and good heart, would have shewn some solicitude about *ladies*, thus singularly frightened,

ened, who could not possibly be involved in the atrocious guilt of my horrible democratical discourse. But no—the tall officer had said, "Go along after your husband, and be d—d;" and perhaps humanity or common civility from any of the shorter officers, after that order, might have been construed *mutiny*.

As we passed along the street musing on the *Agreeable Surprise* (the drama we went to see), a gentleman, who purposely followed us from the Theatre, came up to me in North-street; and after expressing his indignation at what he termed, in the warmth of first impressions, the *cowardly* treatment we had received, offered to be a witness, if I chose to indict the assailants for a breach of the peace. I knew him not. He appeared to be a gentleman, a man of sense, and was of a *liberal profession*. I thanked him very sincerely; and told him, what was strictly true, that I did not know the name of any of the persons in uniform who had caused the outrage; and that it was too soon at present to come to any determination. He gave me his address, and left me politely; with an assurance that, if called upon, he should come forward with zeal, in the cause of truth and justice, to bear witness against such unmerited insult, injury, and oppression. He felt hurt, as a man, for the ill-usage of me and my family; and, as a Briton, for violated law and liberty. He told me he had been in the camp; and I was mistaken if I thought that ALL the officers disapproved my sermon, or would justify the insult that had been offered this night, to punish me for the zeal it displayed in promoting the happiness of human nature. As he was much in the camp, and did not wish to be personally embroiled in disputes, he desired his name might not be mentioned, unless I should determine to prosecute. He is still ready to come forward and give his testimony in a court of justice.

On the day following, that is, on Wednesday the 21st of August, I had resided at Brighton just four weeks, the term for which I had hired my house of Mr. Grantham of Lewes. My friend was to leave the town on the morrow. It was therefore determined that I should accompany him, and hasten with all my baggage-waggons of sedition and treason, to London. I know not whether the Tower was fortified with additional works on

my

my intention being discovered; but to London I went, and Brighton, I suppose, felt itself relieved; like Rome when it had vomited out CATILINE.

At London I had the happiness of meeting many sensible and respectable friends, whose zeal in the present posture of my affairs evinced their sincerity. Their friendship seemed to increase from the indignation they felt at the unmerited treatment I had received. They urged me to publish my sermon; assuring me it would redound to my honour, confute my adversaries, and promote the glorious cause of peace and humanity. Letters of encouragement, and even congratulation, arrived from various quarters, from strangers of the first abilities, who signed their names; and from others who chose to remain in concealment, in times, as they expressed it, like these.

The affair at first could be known only to a few. I had not been in London above two days, before it was stated, with some inaccuracies, but yet upon the whole with much truth, in several of the newspapers which *dared* to relate it. It was some time before the

the ministerial papers were ordered to open their masked batteries of abuse.

A *Lewes* paper, published on the twenty-sixth of August, was shewn me; in which was a very incoherent account of my sermon, with strange and flighty observations upon it. My sentiments and language were misrepresented; but, I believe, without any hostile intention, and solely from errors of memory and judgment. In the midst of a very injurious and mistaken report of my sermon, praises were introduced, which I must consider as hyperbolical. It asserted, that *I spoke with a flow of eloquence scarcely to be equalled!* at the extravagance of which eulogium, I will join in a hearty laugh with my enemies and detractors. This account was in itself worthy of little attention; and derived its importance from its immediate diffusion throughout the neighbouring camp at Brighton, and the subsequent copying of its errors into the London papers. Garbled paragraphs, the most unfavourable and the most untrue, were printed from it, as authentic intelligence from Brighton, in one or two venal publications: All praise was omitted; abuse of the most virulent kind succeeded. I was not indeed surprised at the offence taken at the nonsense and vulgarity which was put into my mouth. From this time it became fashionable, among a certain description of persons, to fill private letters, and embellish conversation, with every calumny and falsehood which could irritate their own party against me, and soften, in the minds of the Public, the improper conduct of the avengers at the Theatre. I have laughed very heartily at the representations which were communicated, in the circles of fashion, to a family of high rank, and intimately connected with the court, concerning the style and contents of my sermon. They told me what they had heard, with great good humour. I ought to have lost their friendship, if what they had heard had been true; but they knew me too well to believe it. I will mention one or two particulars, which they said were generally circulated in that high sphere.—I had described minutely the Prince of Wales's tent; and I had said to the officers, "Pull off your "fine cloaths, and then let us see what you "are." I appeal to the bitterest of my enemies present at the sermon, whether there is the least degree of truth in these ridiculous accounts. It were endless to enumerate the

silly

filly things of this kind which were fathered upon me in converfation. The abfurdeft, yet moft malicious, was, that I faid to the whole *body of privates of the whole camp*, affembled in the church, " You fools you, why do you " obey your commanders, who are only a " parcel of knaves and fycophants?" All who know me will do me the juftice to affert, that I am incapable of fuch vulgar language in a pulpit, and that I never uttered or entertained fentiments fo abfurd and fo mifchievous. All who heard me will, I am confident, reprobrate falfehood fo contemptible, fo malevolent, fo unjuft. Before God and man, in the moft folemn manner, I affirm that no fuch doctrine was inculcated by me or my fermon, or any where elfe, either in thefe words or any other, directly or indirectly. The truth is, that in a very large congregation there were many who perhaps little attended or little underftood the fcope of the fermon; but when it became the fubject of general converfation, all who were there, were willing to retail a little to thofe who were not there. What they under- ftood, or remembered imperfectly, they fup- plied, merely for fomething to fay, by inven- tion. They were unwilling to appear unable to satisfy inquirers. The most ignorant and illiterate found something to say; and thus a thousand most absurd reports originated from *folly*, and the love of talking for talking sake. Malice, however, seized them, stamped them with a counterfeit mark of authenticity, and sent them to pass current in the world, among those who had no opportunities of detecting the imposition. Thus I suffered in the opinion of a part of the Public, whose esteem I should certainly have possessed, if it had known the real intention, the beneficial tendency, the respectful manner, and the Christian sentiments of my discourse.

I will here take the liberty of inserting a few Extracts and Letters, which I received from voluntary correspondents.

*Extract from the unsolicited Letter of a Gentleman whose abilities and learning, as a writer on politics, are held by the Public in high esteem.*

" Consolation would be misplaced. The
" enmity of such wretches is a most honour-
" able distinction; and a minister of religion
" will feel that he has well performed his
                                              " duty,

"duties, when his admonitions have pro-
"voked their rage. Their *wincing* is indeed
"a proof that these men have more conscience,
"or at least shame left, than I supposed."

*Extract from the Letter of a Clergyman whom
I saw present at the Sermon, but a perfect
stranger, except by* NAME *and person.*

"The best vindication would be to publish
"the sermon, and prosecute your assailants
"at the Theatre; and I think the world will
"acquit you of entertaining unfavourable sen-
"timents of the existing government of this
"kingdom."

\*\*\*\* "An enraged son of Mars, the day
"the sermon was preached at Brighton, just
"on my coming out, attacked me as furiously
"as a bull-dog, and wondered why such a
"d——d fellow should be allowed to preach
"at Brighton;—talked of writing to Bishop
"——, Archbishop ——, &c.; enquired
"who was the preacher; branded *me*, now
"and then, with reproach, and used ill lan-
"guage, exceedingly unfit for a gentleman."
(N. B. *This, I have reason to think, happened
in the church.*)

"I an-

" I answered him in short, that the sermon
" was but too true; and that no Bishop what-
" ever would notice any representations, pro-
" vided they were JUST, which could be
" made of it."

" He then took care to circulate a report,
" that I countenanced and defended the ser-
" mon; and, I assure you, I had my doubts,
" but I should have met with some insult
" similar to yours, which you may depend on
" it, I should have resented, by redress from
" that palladium of British liberty, an English
" jury."

*Extract of a Letter from a Friend, whose great
abilities and excellent character are respected
in a large circle of acquaintance.*

" Contradictions of the falsehood circulated
" in the *Free Briton* concerning your dis-
" course, would keep up the stimulus in your
" calumniators.

" Nothing would so effectually silence the
" scoundrels as publishing your sermon; and
" yet SCANDAL WOULD INSINUATE that
" you

" *you had suppressed some passages;* and
" *your meaning in others would be wil-*
" *fully perverted* by the wretches who are
" HIRED to do such DIRTY WORK. These
" fellows would be glad to recommend them-
" selves by abusing you.*****

" You will get some enemies by the spirit
" with which you have defended CHRISTIAN
" HUMANITY against tyrants and murderers.
" But I hope sincerely that you may find the
" love of honest men more than a compensa-
" tion for the malice of the worthless. You
" are sure of the best support, the comfort of
" an approving conscience. THE REST IS
" INSIGNIFICANT. ***** The BITTER-
" NESS OF THE TIMES INCREASES." ****

*Extract from the Letter of a Correspondent at Brighton, whose sense and virtues are worthy of the highest esteem; and who was present at the Sermon, and in the Theatre.*

" I fancy the reptiles have spit their spite,
" done an heroic act before the ladies, and
" will again plume themselves on their valiant
" exploit of disturbing a Theatre." ****

" You

"You are in possession of more than my approbation—of my sincere admiration of your PRINCIPLES, and of your CONDUCT too on the late occasion; nor can the treatment you received from a mercenary tribe, (a small tribe too, remember, not more, I believe, than twenty!—and who were they?) instigated by a desire of PLEASING THE HIGHER POWERS, deprive you of the consciousness of having done *nothing* wrong."

"It is a great, but a disagreeable compliment paid to you. Unnoticed had been a less able attempt to inculcate any doctrine."

---

For the Letter of the Reverend Mr. Mossop, (which was also unsolicited,) curate of the parish of Brighton, who read Prayers, and sat in the desk during my sermon, I must beg leave to refer my Reader to the *Appendix*; where he will find several other papers, omitted in this place for want of room.

The next is from a perfect stranger, who signs his name.

"Sir,

"Permit a stranger, who reads and hears
"the various comments, strictures, and con-
"jectures of various parties, on the unex-
"ampled outrage you suffered at the Theatre
"at Brighton, to urge you to publish the ser-
"mon, with the subsequent circumstances, as
"soon as possible; and to advertise that such
"is your intention. Name your assailants,
"and the regiments they belong to, as far as
"you can positively ascertain them.

"In the "*World*," this day, they admit
"the treatment you have received to be un-
"justifiable. In the paper improperly called
"the *True Briton*, you are censured with a
"severity perfectly characteristic of the des-
"potic party and principles by whom it is
"protected and supported. They seem to
"think, by committing you to your Metro-
"politan, that you will be made an example,
"to deter other honest men from doing their
"duty, and that they may make them the
"*devoted*

"  *devoted victims* of their dreadful cabals and
" intentions. However, Sir, BAD AS TIMES
" ARE, an honest Englishman, doing publicly
" his duty, need neither fear the censure of a
" Bishop nor the frowns of a Prince. ✱✱✱✱
" ✱✱✱✱✱✱.

    " I am,

✱✱✱✱✱,   Your humble servant,
*August* 27.
      ✱✱✱✱✱ ✱✱✱✱✱."

I will add but one more letter: It comes from a person unknown; but as he says he was present at the sermon, it may properly be inserted in this place.

  " Rev. Sir,

" As a fellow-collegian, as a brother cler-
" gyman, and as a hearer of your sermon at
" Brighton, which gave so much offence to
" the Military, but which gave me so much
" pleasure, I take the liberty to trouble you
" with this;—merely to express my earnest
" hope that you will bring to punishment, or
" at least to public notice, those *puppies* who
" insulted you in consequence of their disap-
" probation; and that you will also print
         " your

" your sermon;—being assured that it will
" not only be an AMPLE REFUTATION OF
" CALUMNY, but will also give pleasure to
" every impartial person, and will encrease
" your already well-deserved reputation.——
" \*\*\*\*\*\*\*\*\*\*.

OXFORD,                         " I am, Sir, &c."
Sept. 15.

I have many other Letters full of expressions of approbation, and bearing testimony to the beneficial tendency of my sermon; but I forbear to insert them, lest I should weary my Readers with a repetition. There are many witnesses to the receipt of the above by the post; which I mention, because I am aware that the wicked malevolence of my calumniators will insinuate suspicions of their authenticity. Their writers would willingly come forward, but I would not let their friendship and their honesty expose them to the malice of my adversaries. Many able and impartial Letters on the subject have appeared in the independent newspapers; for which I here make my grateful acknowledgments to the unknown authors, who dared to stand forth volunteers in the defence of injured truth, and of an individual likely to be oppressed by overbearing influence.

But what, I may be asked, could offend the officers? I know not; for I said nothing but what their hearts must accord to, when unbiassed by misunderstanding or misconception. I am enlisted under no party. I espoused only the general interests of humanity. I enforced its dictates by the sanctions of the Christian religion. If I may venture to conjecture the cause of their displeasure, I should suppose that a passion, which Young calls the *universal passion*, was offended at my detracting something from the pomp and parade of military preparation, and the glory of conquest. That passion, when offended, is of all perhaps the most vindictive. That passion might be irritated when, after deploring the calamities of war, I said, that the finery of its externals could not conceal from the eye of humanity its real and shocking deformity. Defensive war, in which alone the militia is concerned, I never censured. Offensive war I did and do reprobate as the disgrace and
cala-

calamity of human nature, and equally repugnant to reason and to the mild and friendly spirit of Christianity. I despise and abominate despotism wherever it exists; but there were *no despots at the church*, there are no despots in England, and therefore my censures of despots could never be considered as a personal invective on any hearer, or any British Potentate. Was it pride then, and vanity, that were hurt? I should hope that generosity in military men would overcome pride, if any existed; that it would prevent a numerous and opulent body, *who have suffered nothing*, and who *are not even named* or known by me at this hour, from endeavouring to injure and ruin, as far as they can, an individual and his *family*; a family which, whatever may be *his* demerits, are certainly innocent, and worthy every man's kindness and protection. As independent as any of my assailants in mind, and perfectly easy in circumstances, I want not their assistance; but they owed me, from their office, protection from violence, if it had been offered from any quarter. I know brave men, grey-headed veterans, whose swords would have

*leaped*

*leaped from their scabbards* to defend a clergyman and a woman from the slightest insult at a public Theatre. How different those who deliberately took counsel together against a clergyman, and assembled in a body, in a narrow passage, to insult him, while they were driving him from the Theatre, and he made no resistance: Who were rude and insolent to a defenceless woman and child; and not contented with this, continued to persecute the insulted party by virulent invectives against them in their absence: Who slunk from public censure, and did not venture to avow, by their names, the act which they gloried to execute when there was no danger of opposition. To call names! the last poor revenge of malicious imbecillity! To suffer misrepresentation to go forth in news-papers uncontradicted, after having sated their revenge by a public outrage! I firmly believe, that the majority of the brave men throughout the army disapprove such conduct, and blush for the degradation of the military character. True magnanimity is never captious; forgives real injuries, is easily satisfied with concession, and
holds

holds out the hand of friendship to a conquered adversary. I made every concession in the Theatre which a gentleman could give, or a gentleman demand; yet I was still pursued with foul names, that would have disgraced a scolding woman of the lowest order.

But that generosity which I have not experienced, I have wished to exercise. I might have discovered their names by diligent investigation; but I have never inquired; and I know no more of them at this moment, than I do of officers among our Sardinian, our Spanish, or our Neapolitan auxiliaries. I might have prosecuted them, but I never meditated such revenge. I leave them to their own reflections, and to the opinion which the unprejudiced part of their own profession must entertain of their conduct. They ought to have made an apology as public as their offence. It would have displayed a noble magnanimity; such, indeed, as cannot be expected from persons capable of *persisting* in mean revenge. Much is to be allowed to the surprise of sudden passion, and to human infirmity. But perseverance in illegal vengeance, when the law is open, is inexcusable in a defender of law and order.

The

The mode of punishment adopted must be improper; because, had my sermon been all that mass of absurdity which either they or their adherents think it right to represent it; yet, as our Church is Episcopal, as our Constitution is inviolate, our Courts of justice pure, a regular process should have been instituted. The accused has then an opportunity of vindicating his innocence. A self-appointed court-martial and a summary process, without giving the culprit leave to defend himself, strikes at the very root of public justice. They who had recourse to it, might themselves suffer by the precedent. All men, all professions, all ranks, are deeply concerned in preventing the prevalence of a summary process without judge or jury. A breach of the peace from its preservers is doubly mischievous. It destroys confidence in the legally appointed defenders against violence. A riot might have ensued from the outrage at the Theatre. If I had thrown myself on the protection of the multitude, who were my friends, the consequence might have been fatal to my aggressors, or to persons unconcerned. It is some aggravation of their furious onset, that they had *an army of many thousands* within a *few* a *few minutes march* of the spot. How dangerous the experiment of risking a riot in such a cause, and in such a place! And if the consciousness of irresistible power gave confidence, how ungenerous, against adversaries so defenceless, was such confidence! With arms by my side, with confederates at my back, and whole regiments within my call, I would scorn to attack any unarmed individual; much less one in a profession forbidden defence by arms, and naturally seeking of the generous soldier that protection which it cannot, consistently with decorum, secure to itself by force. My enemies triumphed over me. But amidst all the exultation of their triumph, I would not exchange situations with them. In such a rencontre I had rather be the assaulted than the assailant. The laurels gained in victories like these are but blushing honours.

I was defeated, but not depressed. The generous public have shown me many marks of approbation. My most valuable friends have come forward in my support, with a zeal and steadiness of attachment which would cheer the drooping heart under persecutions infinitely severer than any which I have endured.

They have indeed confoled me in the midſt of ſcurrility. But above all, my own mind has confoled me. The cauſe which I ſupported with an honeſt zeal, and, as it appears, with effect, was a good cauſe. I glory in the cauſe. I will never retract a ſentence that I uttered in maintaining it. Under every affliction, and in the arms of death, it ſhall be my comfort, that I laboured ſtrenuouſly, and in *my proper ſphere*, to ſtop the effuſion of human blood, and to promote peace on earth, and good-will among all that are dignified by the name and the form of MAN, however divided by oceans, or diſtinguiſhed by languages, or detached by forms of government, differently modified, according to their own choice.

But why do I not publiſh my ſermon? Before I anſwer that queſtion I muſt do myſelf the juſtice to aſſure the Public, that I had no knowledge of a little Pamphlet, which I am informed was publiſhed under the title of Dr. Knox's Sermon. It was beneath ſuch formal and ſerious notice as would have been neceſſary to have ſtopt its ſale. I found it a mere tranſcript from an article in a newſpaper, which had been ſome time publiſhed, and which

which hardly filled a column. It carried with it its own marks of want of authenticity. Enemies, as well as friends, must immediately have discerned that it was nothing more than a mere contrivance of some industrious artizan to raise himself a trifling supply, by imposing on the public curiosity. The purpose, I think, must have been defeated by the clumsy execution of the projector. I slightly mention it now, and caution the Public against the delusion, because I find that zealous partisans have been base enough to hand it about, with an assurance that it was genuine. How do truth, justice, and benevolence fall before the spirit of party! Political frenzy, inflamed by interest and ambition, seems to trample on all the limits of right and wrong; and men, honest in their nature and honest in their lives and conversation, become temporary knaves in the struggles of political contest. I affirm, that no man who asserted the catchpenny pamphlet to be mine, believed it.

But the question recurs, Why do I not publish my sermon? My reply is, that I do not think it would answer the expectation which the irrational opposition to it has excited,

excited, and that it was not written for publication. I sought peace. I never took one step to inflame the minds of the people. If I had chosen to publish my sermon, I am told it would have been rapidly diffused over the kingdom. It was every where expected with impatience. Whether it would have had a powerful effect or not, let those judge who heard it. I wished sincerely to avoid the fomenting of troubles and commotion; and I suffered a sermon (calculated in my own opinion only to diffuse a love of peace and mankind) to sleep on its shelf, lest, by opposing many stubborn prejudices which unfortunately prevail at the present moment, I might disturb my own tranquillity, without promoting my grand object, public peace. I do not engage not to publish it. It is at hand ready for the press, and shall make its appearance, if I see it likely to effect its sole purpose, that of doing good by teaching universal benevolence, inspiring a love of peace, good government and order. Prejudice at present might impede its beneficial effect.

This answer to the question why I do not publish my sermon, is addressed solely to my friends.

friends. My enemies do not clamour for its publication so much as my friends, and for a good reason. Those among them who have heard it, must know, that its publication would evince that their outrageous displeasure, as well as their consequent violence, was totally unjustifiable. It would shew their SUPERIORS of how little value has been their ardour in this boasted service. Staunch champions as they are for loyalty, they would appear to have attacked the territories of a friend and an ally. It would be evident that there had been a prodigal waste of valour. They would find themselves qualified to say, in the words of the old song, " Oh, we have " been fighting where there were no wars." What notice or what reward could be claimed or expected, when it should appear, as they know it would, that they had been attacking one who had been on the late occasion, as many years before, contending in the service of his King and Country; and of one who had *attempted* more public services to both by his labours, than some even of themselves, who perhaps may not have had equal opportunities or equal success, in making their beneficial

neficial exertions oftensible. They would find, if they were led by his sermon to inspect his other lucubrations, that he has in many of them, to the best of his poor abilities, paid honour to the King and defended the Constitution; though " *non tali auxilio*," he confesses, may be applied to his defence  They would find, imperfect as his endeavours have been, that they have for many years been extending, not only over the British empire, but to most of those foreign countries which speak or cultivate the British language. It is indeed certain the antagonists were not *bound* to know this; for it would be *despotism indeed* to compel men to read, or force them either, *invitâ Minervâ*, or *invitis ipsis*, to be acquainted with the literary republic, or to pay any regard to the state of literature. Much clergy is not necessary when men combat arguments with force. CEDAT TOGA ARMIS, is a glorious motto, in spite of that blockhead, Cicero, who was no soldier, and made but a poor figure indeed, when his head and hands were cut off by the HERO, Mark Anthony, and nailed on the pulpit, where he had displayed his offensive eloquence. A glorious

rious triumph of the sword over the tongue; of brute force over genius, taste, philosophy, elegance, humanity, and wit! What are these to swords and battle-axes?

No—it is impossible, as there are many proofs on record, that I am, and have ever been, a peaceable member of the community, a friend to order, a lover of my King and Country; it is impossible that any honour or emolument could be bestowed by the *Givers of good things*, as a remuneration for forcing me to fall back by a RETREAT that is now almost as famous as the retreat of the ten thousand under General Xenophon. No reflection on that General! besides, if it were, I should be forgiven; for really, Gentlemen, (pray believe me,) he was not in English pay, but a foreigner and an antient, in a country called Greece, a good way from Brighthelmstone. In speaking of Xenophon I cannot possibly allude to any of my conquerors.

But I beg pardon for the short digression. I was saying that the publication of my sermon would make it appear, that the *inquisitorial detachment* of forces deserved no reward for their strenuous services, thus vilely thrown away against a voluntary friend to every thing which they are *paid* by us to defend. My sermon was a defence of peace, order, law; their attack an illegal and useless violation of them all.

Away with the sordid idea! I will not for one moment believe, what has been frequently suggested to me, that these persons, whoever they were (for I know no more of them than our good friend the Pope at Rome), were incited to display their prowess and patriotism in the Brighton Theatre, in the hope of pleasing a great Personage, resident in that Town, to whom, as that common liar common Fame reports, some of them immediately repaired after the terrible sermon, and told their tale. Wretchedly mistaken must they have been to think, if they did think, which cannot be true, to rise in favour of a gracious superior, and procure in future, at court, honour or promotion, by oppressing an individual in the exercise of his lawful profession, for doing his duty faithfully in the parish church, and recommending that Christian religion, that love of peace, and that good order in which the gracious superior must delight, or he would cease to be gracious.

No,

No, no; I have a far better opinion of him than they had, if they thought so. It was a foolish speculation, to think of claiming to themselves the merit of *an exclusive loyalty*, and deriving honour and rewards for it, by disturbing the public peace. It could not be so. The gracious superior must have laughed them to scorn, when they detailed to him the action at the Theatre at Brighton, if, while considering their claims, he compared them with those of hardy veterans who were at the same moment opposing the terrible armies of France. There can be no truth in the suggestion; and if there were, the publication of my sermon must destroy all hopes at once, and make them fall to the ground like a battered redoubt. It would appear immediately, that they had made all this fuss in combating only a *supposed* enemy—a pasteboard Sans Culotte—stuck up to shoot bullets at, for want of better sport, *right earnest flesh and blood;*—a mere phantom, caused by the fever of loyalty run mad, and patriotism in a trance. No, Madam FAME, though thou hast a thousand tongues, and all of them hung upon swivels, thou shalt never persuade me, that the meanest mortal that ever wore a red coat could possibly think to recommend himself to the higher powers by routing, in a body, an unresisting clergyman and his wife. NOTORIETY, however desirable in itself, so obtained would be like the notoriety of a man standing on the pillory;—a *disagreeable service*, but which would seldom entitle the party to *honourable* distinction or advancement out of it. I only mention this illiberal suggestion, as one instance to prove how little dependance is to be placed on common report, in times when party-spirit runs high; and when many are in the hope of getting a loaf or a fish, by hook or by crook, in shewing their own zeal to men in power; and misrepresenting and driving all others away, lest they should want to go snacks, and so, by the multitude of guests, lessen the good cheer. Political PSEUDOLOGY, as it is called by the learned, is too much studied of late, and is but too successful. But I will not believe, either that British officers could misrepresent a fact for the purpose of ingratiating themselves with a superior; or that a superior would listen one moment to a tale that tended to injure, in his opinion,

opinion, a peaceful individual, known for his attachment to the purest state of the constitution.

No; I honour the King and the Prince; and I firmly believe that they would scorn to persecute or to oppress, at the instigation of the most OPULENT PEER in the realm, the most defenceless individual, the most abject outcast, the most forlorn beggar in the British empire. I may be abused, reviled, forced out of Theatres, but no man shall rob me of my loyalty. The Father of his people shall ever find me a dutiful son; and the Prince himself shall not excel me as a peaceable subject, and a friend to law and order. Though he is certainly in all other qualities as much above me, as he is in birth, rank, and the glorious prospect of one day ruling over a great, enlightened, and a free people, he shall not excel me in a zeal for the interests of my Country and of the human race.

O Loyalty! O Law! O the Constitution! O Liberty!—(yes, I *will* add LIBERTY; for liberty is *constitutional* in England, and no man dares to deny it)—how I love you!— You are the parents of peace, plenty, learning, arts, commerce, every thing truly desirable.

able. I love you all dearly for this; aye, and I love you for something else too; for if it had not been for you, O LAW, I should have stood but a bad chance in the memorable action of Brighton Theatre. Then " God " bless the King and preserve the Constitu- " tion." It is not the prayer of patriotism only; but also of cordial gratitude. For if the King and the Constitution had not inter- fered, perhaps I should not have been able to pray for them at this moment. In some countries I should have been *stilettoed* in that horrible dark passage there, behind the boxes, a place fit for assassination. I do not think I should have come so well off, as I did, among our good friends the *Neapolitan soldiers*. The Austrians would have made very short work of it. But IN ENGLAND!—*blessed Isle!*—I will daily thank my God, upon my knees, for the happiness of being born in a free coun- try— the King covered me with a helmet, the Constitution with a shield, and the Law with a coat of mail. I marched through my ene- mies unhurt, for the *law* and the King, under Providence, were my guards. Hard names break no bones; and though the tongue is a sharp weapon, yet it does not perforate the skin. The drum of the ear, like the regimental drum, *that wonderful agent on the rational soul,* is made of tough materials; and indeed, though it cannot, like that great inspirer of courage, make a great noise, yet it can bear a good deal, or it had been broken. Certain it is, that in the exploit of the twentieth of August, I was under peculiar obligations to the King and the Constitution. Then you will not wonder at my repeating so soon, God bless the King, and preserve the Constitution in health and vigour. They shall ever continue to be my favourite toast; and I will add to them the CHURCH, though I never should get any thing in it, but expulsion from the Play-house, and a volley of military ANATHEMAS, which, by the way, I think are quite as good in their effect, and somewhat similar, though not quite so profane, as the cursing and swearing of his Holiness at the Vatican. Foul words, however, only shew the foulness of the source whence they flow; they do not defile the object of them, like mud thrown upon a white stocking. Like a *dirty* action, they only befoul the doer of it.

Indeed, as a thunder-bolt attends thunder, so they sometimes are accompanied with blows, and thrusts, and gashes, and tramplings, and *simple manslaughter;* especially if they succeed in *setting a mob against a man, by calling him obnoxious names in public,* as they call a dog mad when they want to get him hanged. But the King and the Constitution prevented the hard words from growing, in their natural progress, to hard deeds; and here I am, and my wife and children too, by our comfortable fireside, safe and sound;—thanks to the King and Constitution, under God. Then play up, MUSIC, "*God save the King;*" and I will say, *Amen, Amen, and Amen:* and, GOD SAVE THE PEOPLE too; for what is a King without the people? But give me leave to desire the musicians, while their hands are in, to make an anthem immediately, for Sundays at least, of the words,

"GLORY TO GOD IN THE HIGHEST, AND
"ON EARTH PEACE, GOOD-WILL TO-
"WARDS MEN."

If this is sedition, let the Attorney-General, or a Court-Martial, revise the Bible, and blot out the texts prohibited. Dreadful sedition may lurk

lurk in that old Book, though the Brightonian phalanx might not know it. If they had, they would have feized the church Bible, and carried it to be burnt by the hands of the common hangman, as foon as he had FETTERED *me*.

The repetition of the *text* reminds me of my horrible fermon, which, wonderful to relate, though full of *poifon*, flowed from thefe very words, (all fweet as they are, and *falubrious*,) as naturally as the ftreamlet in the meadow from the native fountain. If any of *my* words are feditious or treafonable, I will eat them. That's fair; though I own there is fcarcely any food which agrees fo ill with the ftomach. But I would venture a wager, if I were in the habit of laying wagers, that let all the Attorney-Generals in Chriftendom, turn and twift, and twift and turn them, with their fpectacles on their nofes, as long as they pleafe, even till the French are brought back to their old Conftitution, and the Baftile rebuilt; and they fhall not find one fyllable of fedition or treafon from the text to the laft inference. They fhall, after reading them forwards, read them backwards, like the Hebrews; and then upwards and downwards,

like

like the Chinese; and then crossways, like Bonnell Thornton; and if they find any treason in them, I will give them my skin to make parchment of, and warrant it whole, notwithstanding the celebrated rencontre in which, had not the King and Constitution interfered, it might have been pierced like a cullender.

But the subject of my sermon recurs. The Ministerial prints have given pretended quotations from it: I am sure the authors of those prints never saw it, and therefore their quotations must be from memory. Great wits have short memories; and of course great powers of invention. No wonder, therefore, that the quotations are considerably different from the real and genuine composition: they are indeed sadly mutilated; the poor bantlings are so disfigured by ill-usage, that I can hardly recognise any resemblance. I may, I think, fairly conclude, that, as the papers called the *True Briton* and the *Sun*, and fifty more perhaps throughout the kingdom, have selected them, they are intended to exhibit the passages which gave offence. I will therefore quote the original sentences to which they relate, copied literally from my sermon.
They

They are all, I believe, comprehended in the following detached paragraphs; which I select, *not from any preference*, but *solely* because they have been fixed upon by the adversaries, and published by them in a most imperfect state.

" Let it be deemed by CHRISTIANS a
" greater honour to pluck one sprig of olive,
" than to bring home whole loads of laurel;
" —to be welcomed by the cordial salutes
" of hearts delighted with the blessings of
" PEACE RESTORED, than by the forced ex-
" plosion of ten thousand cannons, and the false
" brilliancy of a venal illumination." *****

" Ye also in the lowest ranks of society,
" wherever ye are dispersed all over the ha-
" bitable globe; ye, our poor brethren, who
" are *numbered but not named* when ye fall
" for your respective countries; who, in fo-
" reign climes, happily not in our own,
" are looked down upon with sovereign con-
" tempt, and even let out by petty despots,
" as butchers of your species, in any cause,
" for pay, PRESERVE AT LEAST YOUR RE-
" LIGION; obey its laws, hope for its com-
" forts; bind it round your hearts; and let
" neither

"neither the artful philosopher, by his false
"refinements, beguile you, nor the haughty
"oppressor, by keeping you in total igno-
"rance, rob you of this treasure; it is a *pearl
"of great price*; lock it up in the casket of
"your bosoms, there to remain through life,
"inviolate; it is your only riches; but it
"makes you opulent in the midst of poverty,
"and happy in the midst of woes, which,
"without it, would be scarcely tolerable."****

———

" If the Christian religion in all its purity,
"and in its FULL FORCE, were suffered to
"prevail universally, the sword of offensive
"war must be sheathed for ever, and the din
"of arms would at last be silenced in perpe-
"tual peace. Glorious idea!—I might be
"pardoned, if I indulged the feelings of en-
"thusiastic joy at a prospect so transporting.
"PERPETUAL AND UNIVERSAL PEACE!—
"the jubilee of all human nature! Pardon
"my exultation, if it be only an illusive pro-
"spect. Though the vision is fugacious as
"the purple tints of an evening sky, it is en-
"chanting; it is innocent, as it is delightful.
"The very thought furnishes a rich banquet
"for Christian benevolence.

" But

"But let us pause in our expressions of joy; for when we turn from the fancied elysium to sad reality, to scenes of blood and desolation, we are the more shocked by the dismal contrast. Let us then leave ideal pictures; and consider a moment the most rational means of promoting, as far as in our power, *perpetual and universal peace.* If war be a scourge, as it has been ever called and allowed to be, it must be inflicted for our offences. Then let every one, in every rank, the most elevated as well as the most abject, endeavour to propitiate the Deity, by innocence of life and obedience to the divine law, that the scourge may no longer be necessary. Let him add his prayers to his endeavours, that devastation may no more waste the ripe harvest, (while many pine with hunger,) burn the peaceful village, level the hut of the harmless cottager, overturn the palace, and deface the temple; destroying, in its deadly progress, the fine productions of art as well as of nature:—but that the shepherd's pipe may warble in the vale, where the shrill clarion and the drum's dissonance now grate "harshly

" harshly on the ear of humanity;—that *peace*
" *may be within and without our walls*, and
" plenteousness in our cottages as well as in
" our palaces;—that we may learn to rejoice
" in *subduing* ourselves, our PRIDE, *whence*
" *cometh contention*, and all other malignant
" passions, rather than in REDUCING FAIR
" CITIES TO ASHES, and erecting a blood-
" stained streamer in triumph over those
" who may be fallen indeed—but fallen in
" defending with bravery, even to death,
" their wives, their children, their houses, and
" their altars, from the destroying dæmon of
" offensive war."

All the above passages have, I believe, been partially and ignorantly cited, at various times, in various diurnal publications, so as to render them scarcely intelligible.

I concluded my sermon with the following Prayer, which has been pretty faithfully represented in some of the more candid papers, but, at the same time, abbreviated.

" O thou God of mercy, grant that the
" sword may return to its scabbard forever,
" that the religion of Jesus Christ may be
" duly

" duly underſtood, and its benign influence
" powerfully felt, by all kings, princes, ru-
" lers, nobles, counſellors, and legiſlators on
" the whole earth,—that they may all com-
" bine, in a league of philanthropy, to en-
" force by reaſon and mild perſuaſion, the
" law of love, or Chriſtian charity, among
" all mankind, in all climes, and in all ſects;
" conſulting, like ſuperior beings, the good
" of thoſe beneath them;—not endeavour-
" ing to promote their own power and ag-
" grandizement by force and arms,—but
" building their thrones and eſtabliſhing their
" dominion on the hearts of their reſpective
" people, preſerved from the horrors of war
" by their prudence and clemency; and en-
" joying, exempt from all unneceſſary bur-
" thens, the fruits of their own induſtry;
" —every nation thus bleſt, permitting all
" others under the canopy of Heaven to en-
" joy the ſame bleſſings, uninterrupted, in
" equal peace and ſecurity.

" O melt the hard heart of pride and am-
" bition, that it may ſympathiſe with the
" loweſt child of poverty. And grant, O
" thou God of order, as well as of mercy
" and

"and love, that we of this happily constituted nation may never experience the curse of despotism on one hand; nor, on the other, the cruel evils of anarchy; that as our understandings become enlightened by science, our hearts may be softened by humanity; that we may be ever free, not using our liberty as a cloak for licentiousness; that we may all, in every rank and degree, live together peaceably in Christian love, and die in Christian hope; and that all nations which the Sun irradiates in his course, united in the bonds of amity, may unite also in the joyful acclamation of the text, with heart and voice, and say,— *Glory to God in the highest, on earth peace, good-will towards men.*"

Such, I declare in the most solemn manner, in the face of Heaven and earth, was the general tendency of my whole sermon; a sermon which, in its consequences, has alarmed my family, given trouble to my friends, and exposed me to the venomous shafts of slander. But I scorn complaint, and mean nothing but just representation. I claim not the least merit

rit in the compofition of the fermon. It was almoſt extemporaneous. My enemies allowed that I delivered it feelingly; and indeed it did come from my heart. That was all its merit. My error, if there was any, was the error of my head; a zeal in a good caufe, not checked by the cold reſtraints of worldly policy.

I will endeavour to recapitulate the heads of my difcourfe with brevity. I was guided by my text, and adhered to it clofely. My remarks were not perfonal. I fpoke of peace and war in general. I cenfured neither *our* Government nor *our* Army. I urged the neceffity of piety to God among the *Great*, in an age, when a mighty people, whether with fufficient reafon I knew not, were accufed of *Atheifm*. I particularly recommended Chriſtianity, for its beneficial effects on civil fociety. This led me to the fecond topic, *Peace*. I defcribed, as I felt in imagination, the miferies of the SEAT OF WAR. I endeavoured to diveſt *war* of thofe affumed fplendours, and that appearance of gaiety and happinefs, which do not belong to it, but which feduce the unthinking to view it as a PASTIME. I proceeded to the third point, *Good-will towards men;* and endeavoured to check that vanity and diffipation, which, feeking to make a figure, and ftudying felfifh gratification, forgets the duties of philanthropy, forgets that all men are the fons of one father; and can hear or read of the flaughter of thoufands and tens of thoufands, and of anguifh unutterable, in the field of battle, with joy or indifference; while it weeps over the diftreffes of a novel, or the fictitious woes of a tragedy. I endeavoured to recommend to cabinets and legiflatures, *not to our own in particular*, but to ALL in the civilized world, the *principles* of gofpel charity, as the beft principles of every government and found ftate-policy. I pleaded the caufe of the POOR, and the diftreffed and oppreffed in all countries;—and, if it pleafe God to give me health, I will continue to plead the fame caufe, without fee or reward— *dum Spiritus hos regit artus*,—believing it to be my COMMISSION and duty, as a clergyman, to preach peace and philanthropy, as much as it is the foldier's commiffion and duty to wage war faithfully, and PROTECT THE INJURED ON ALL OCCASIONS, by all LAWFUL means, when he has once entered into the military profeffion.

If

If for this I muſt ſuffer calumny, deſertion, perſecution, I am content. The cauſe ſhall teach me to bear the conſequence cheerfully. My fellow-creatures will do me the juſtice to remember, that I ſhall ſuffer for *being their advocate*, totally unconnected with party, cheerfully renouncing, in this conduct, all views of preferment, of ſordid intereſt, or mean ambition. Happy in a plentiful competence, and a contented mind, I aſk no increaſe, I fear no diminution. Thus independent, I will ever ſpeak my ſentiments with freedom, when called upon by my duty. They are all friendly to man, all favourable to my country; therefore they will bear avowal, and require no ſervile and ſelfiſh reſerve. Nor is this a ſyſtem of conduct *newly* adopted. In aſſerting a ſpirit of independence, imbibed from an early ſtudy of the Greek and Roman hiſtory, I have at leaſt been conſiſtent. Let thoſe decide, who have honoured me with reading what I have written in my retirement, or with hearing what I have preached to the inhabitants of my little hamlet, whether I have not laboured to promote the happineſs of both reader and hearer, by faithfully defending the cause of truth on all subjects on which I have written or spoken, without time-serving, or a sordid and cowardly reserve. My zeal has, doubtless, been often a mistaken zeal; but it has been always an honest zeal. My party is the party of humanity. Influenced by that party, and that alone, I was zealous on a late occasion, in my proper sphere, and in the lawful exercise of my profession, to prevent war by the mild arts of persuasion. Feeble arts indeed, especially in my hands! but I am still equally zealous in the same glorious cause. It is the cause of God and man. And if I could succeed in serving it in the smallest degree, if it were only in turning the minds of men in power, throughout all belligerent nations, to think duly on the subject, I should deem it a greater honour than a triumph, a statue, a ribbon, a coronet, or even a triple mitre. Coats of arms I value not; but let my motto be through life, " Glory to God on high, on earth peace, " good-will towards men." The olive branch shall be my emblem, *et sub hoc signo vincam*. I retired, indeed, from superior numbers in the Theatre, on the same principles which

im-

impelled the Duke of Brunswick to retreat from Jemappe, the Duke of York from Dunkirk, and Prince Cobourg from Maubeuge. But like them, pardon my presumption in pretending a resemblance, I scorned to relinquish the cause. From necessity I surrendered my seat in the box, on the first summons; because the summons was followed up with a force which no individual could successfully oppose. But I surrendered not the free-born mind, and the rights which I possess from this happy Constitution. The unlawful attack of conscious power confirmed me more in my dislike of force usurping the place of argument, and in my settled abhorrence of all modes and degrees of tyranny. I acknowledge myself defeated, but not confuted; compelled to yield my seat, but not my opinion. My conquerors will find it much more difficult to prove to the world, that war is not one of the greatest calamities of human nature, than it was to extrude him, who asserted it to be so, in the PULPIT, from a place that he had purchased for himself and family, at a public and licensed Theatre. It is easier to break the law, than to prove that it ought to be broken. The point of a bayonet may produce a temporary silence and submission, in him whose duty it is to preach what he reads in the gospel; but it cannot erase from that gospel, "*Love your enemies,*"—"*Blessed are the peace-makers,*"—"*Do unto others as you wish they should do unto you,*" and many other passages, tending to unite the hearts of all men in love and union. The prophet Isaiah, certainly a bold preacher, ventures to say, "NATION SHALL NOT LIFT UP SWORD AGAINST NATION; NEITHER SHALL THEY LEARN WAR ANY MORE;" which, were I a liege-born subject of Turkey or Algiers, of Monomotapa or Monomugi, I might contend, is libellous, scandalous, mutinous, seditious, and rebellious. Were I a native of the South Sea Islands, I would send it to the Attorney General of *Owhyee*. I would pull the preacher from the pulpit, if I were a CANNIBAL. But enjoying, as I do, the blessing of living in a free country, a Christian country, and under a King no less remarkable for his attachment to the Christian religion, than his native mildness and philanthropy, I will contend, that all those fine sentences in the sacred

sacred volume, conduce at once to the glory of God who gave them, to the prosperity of the states that maintain them, and to the honour and happiness of human nature, wherever they are *permitted* to prevail. I hope *military force* will never be used to prevent their prevalence. I hope they will ultimately prevail against all *military force;* and that the time may come, under their influence, when mortars, cannons, howitzers, shells, balls, bullets, muskets, fusees, bayonets, long swords, short swords, broad swords, will only be shewn as curiosities in the collection of some antiquarian virtuoso, while spectators shall wag their heads and say with smiles, " How foolish were our
" forefathers to use so much ingenuity in
" the arts of destroying life, when DEATH
" is driving on his triumphal car, and every
" MOMENT crushing with his wheels, or
" mowing with his scythe, youth, beauty,
" strength, grandeur, science, genius, virtue,
" and piety, with undistinguishing and re-
" sistless fury. How much wiser we who
" have learned to beat *their* swords into
" ploughshares, and *their* spears into pruning
" hooks. It was the Gospel which effected
" this

" this happy change. *Man* no longer views
" *man* as his enemy. He exerts the strength
" of his body in *subduing* the earth; his mind
" in arts, sciences, in every thing which
" adorns, refines, and sweetens his *brief* ex-
" istence. His affections, no longer exaspe-
" rated by considering his fellow-creature as
" his destroyer, are all bland, and gentle and
" kind; and he feels and communicates joy
" and comfort to all who are within the
" sphere of his activity. Foolish ancestors!
" studying the arts of destroying and impo-
" verishing each other, when the world is
" wide enough, and fertile enough, to contain
" us all, and make us happy, and as merry
" as our hearts can hold. THE FOLLY OF
" WAR, in old times, might constitute one of
" the best topics for our merry-makings, if it
" were not tinged a little too much with the
" dismal and the tragical."

May the gospel be faithfully preached, and produce this revolution. But the attempt is premature; the time is not yet come, says an objector. It will never come, say I, unless we labour in our vocation to accelerate its arrival. In the scripture-language we are taught to do our duty "*in season and out of season;*" and not be restrained by fear, or by worldly politics, from promoting the benign purposes of the kingdom of heaven. We must not be *traitors to the King of heaven* in the fear of retarding our own preferment at a human court. *What shall it profit?*

But let us not think too badly of the times; for there are who have boldly laboured to promote the gospel doctrines of peace in spite of worldly politics, and those too in a high and honourable station. The Bishop of Llandaff will, I hope, pardon me for taking the liberty of quoting from him some passages in a sermon printed, among others, in octavo, in the year 1788, and published by Mr. Thomas Evans of Paternoster-Row. In page 111 of that volume, commence the following passages, worthier of attention, as far as I can judge, than any thing which my mediocrity was able to advance in the church of Brighton.

" Were all the nations of the earth," says that able Prelate, " converted to the Christian " religion, and the individuals of those na- " tions not *nominal* merely, but *real Chri-* " *stians,*

"*stians*, it would be utterly impossible for a
" state of war EVER to have a beginning
" amongst them. But unhappily for man-
" kind, neither of these events is likely soon
" to take place. Christianity hath amended
" the lives, and elevated the hopes, of a few
" individuals, but has it FULLY AND VIR-
" TUALLY PERVADED THE HEARTS AND
" COUNCILS OF PRINCES, FROM WHENCE
" ARE THE ISSUES OF PEACE AND WAR?"

" The councils of princes are usually go-
" verned either by the princes themselves, or
" by a few individuals of their own appoint-
" ment, who being in most countries free
" from human animadversion, and the fear
" of punishment, too frequently suppose them-
" selves superior to all controul. Men of this
" stamp, if they do not look upon religion as
" a human contrivance, invented by statesmen
" to keep the ignorant in awe, are apt to con-
" sider its influence as limited to the *concerns*
" *of private life*. The prosperity of the state,
" or, which with *them* is the *same thing*, the
" *gratification of their ambition*, or any other
" PASSION, they think may be prosecuted by
" ALL POSSIBLE MEANS; in public transac-
" tions

"tions they acknowledge no justice, but what
"springs from *utility*, and is regulated there-
"by.\*\*\*\*\*\*There can be no doubt that indi-
"viduals, with principles such as these, ARE
"NOT CHRISTIANS. THEY MAY BE PO-
"TENT PRINCES, EXPERIENCED STATES-
"MEN, ABLE GENERALS; BUT THEY ARE
"NOT CHRISTIANS.

"Christianity in its regards, steps beyond
"the *narrow bounds of national advantage,* in
"QUEST OF UNIVERSAL GOOD. It does
"not encourage *particular patriotism* in op-
"position to GENERAL BENIGNITY; or
"prompt us to *love our country* at the EX-
"PENCE OF OUR INTEGRITY; or allow us
"to indulge our *passions* to the *detriment of*
"*thousands*. It looks upon all the human race,
"*as children of* THE SAME FATHER, *and*
"*wishes them* EQUAL *blessings*. In ordering
"us to do good, to LOVE AS BRETHREN,
"to forgive injuries, and to *study peace, it*
"*quite annihilates the disposition for martial*
"*glory*, and utterly DEBASES THE POMP OF
"WAR.\*\*\*\*\*\*

"Brave and unfortunate islanders! (the Cor-
"sicans,) ye stemmed, for a time, the torrent

" of tyranny, in hopes that some of the states
" of Europe would have enabled you to repel
" it with success. YE SHED WITH ARDOUR
" YOUR BEST BLOOD AT THE SHRINE OF
" FREEDOM. Overpowered at length, de-
" sponding, and deserving of a better fate, ye
" fell;—lamented by every friend of hu-
" manity, *assisted by* NONE.

" Was it the *spirit of Christianity* which
" *combined* in an *unnatural union*, three of
" the most POWERFUL SOVEREIGNS IN
" EUROPE, and induced them to plan and
" effectuate the dismemberment of *Poland?*
" ******We ourselves paid no attention either
" to Corsica or Poland,—we either had not a
" disposition, or were not in a condition. We
" were, by some means or other, prevented
" from standing forth the protectors of these
" two devoted countries. Other nations may
" be in a like situation with respect to us;
" and a FEW ARBITRARY PRINCES OF THE
" CONTINENT, who LOOK UPON THEIR
" PEOPLE AS BRUTAL PROPERTY, their
" KINGDOMS AS PRIVATE ESTATES, their
" ministers as STEWARDS, and STANDING
" ARMIES AS COLLECTORS OF THEIR
                                    " RENTS,

"RENTS, MAY CONSPIRE TOGETHER TO
"ANNIHILATE THE LITTLE REMAINING
"LIBERTY OF EUROPE, and yet preserve a
"BALANCE OF DESPOTISM among them-
"selves.******

"Was it the SPIRIT OF CHRISTIANI-
"TY which has prompted, not *African*, but
"EUROPEAN PRINCES, to TRAFFICK IN
"BLOOD, to make a profit of the BUTCHERY
"OF THEIR PEOPLE? Gracious God! whence
"is it that MAN, the noblest of thy terrestrial
"works, can so far forget the *dignity of his*
"*nature*, become so deaf to every CALL OF
"HUMANITY, as to MURDER those who never
"*injured him* or his country, never gave him
"or his country occasion of offence?

"——IBI PAS, UBI PLURIMA MERCES.

"I hope it will not be thought indecorous
"to have spoken thus freely concerning such
"*practices of* SOVEREIGN PRINCES, as appear
"TO BE WHOLLY REPUGNANT TO THAT
"GOSPEL BY WHICH, AND BY WHICH
"ALONE, THEY and WE must look for salva-
"tion and eternal life. The hour may be at
"hand to some of us, it cannot be far off
"from

" from any, when this tremendous truth will
" be better underſtood. In the mean time,
" IT IS OUR (the clergy's) ESPECIAL DUTY,
" to repreſent the RIGHTS OF HUMANITY as
" of far more value than the ARTS OF SOVE-
" REIGNTY; THE LAWS OF CHRISTIANITY
" as far more ſacred than the CUSTOMS of
" civil ſociety."

\*\*\*\*\*\* " This, you will think, is plain
" ſpeaking," continues the Biſhop. " The
" PLACE FROM WHICH IT IS SPOKEN
" REQUIRES PLAIN SPEAKING AT ALL
" TIMES; on a day eſpecially of ſolemn hu-
" miliation for our ſins, you would not expect
" to hear any lax, temporizing principles of
" morality from the PULPIT. Alas! let us
" ſpeak as plainly as we can, we have no
" great expectation of being regarded.\*\*\*\*\*\*
" SELFISHNESS has baniſhed HONESTY; and
" CHRISTIANITY, becauſe it will not *truckle*
" to our paſſions or our intereſts, has loſt all
" its hold on our conſciences."—\*\*\*\*

I muſt quote no more for want of room.
The reader, who, I hope, wiſhes for it all, muſt
be referred to a ſermon preached before the
Univerſity of Cambridge, by R. Watſon, D. D.
F. R. S.

F. R. S. Lord Bishop of Llandaff, and the King's Professor of Divinity in the University of Cambridge. It is the fifth in the octavo volume of his sermons, collected and published by himself in 1788, *republished* eight years after it was preached, and therefore no sudden effusion. It is an honour to Episcopacy.

My sermon, compared with his Lordship's, as to freedom of expression, is *courtier-like*. I have not been able to follow either his precept or his example. What if his Lordship had preached it before the military inquisition in Brighton church, instead of the *University of Cambridge?* Why, you will say, that if he had been profane enough to have gone to the Play-house two or three days afterwards, as I was, the said inquisition, or their delegates, would have *torn his lawn sleeves for him,* and perhaps have called him a Scoundrel, a Rascal, and a Democrat. Now I say no, Sir; no such thing. They would not have torn his lawn sleeves. Though the Bishop's sermon would have been infinitely *more provoking,* inasmuch as it is infinitely more excellent than mine, they would have behaved to him with respect, or the politeness characteristic of their

their profession. Such champions do not attack members of the House of Lords. Me they thought they might annihilate, if they pleased; me, one of the lowest of the clergy, at the bottom of the profession; a mere private, one of the *rank and file*. Before the Revolution in France, great people used to drive over little people in the streets of Paris, crush them to atoms, and say no more than, " Drive on, coachman, it is only a Sans " Culotte; there are enough left." Now " *they order these matters better in England:*" Thanks TO THE KING AND CONSTITUTION; yea! blessed be those laws which preserve a clergyman, without a cassock to his back, from the sword of the violent, with as much care and tenderness for him as for the lawn sleeves of the mitred sage.

Now I do not wish to make his Lordship *particeps criminis*; but as he, on the same subject, and before a whole University, whence his sentiments must flow in channels in all directions over the kingdom, went much greater lengths than I did, and met with applause, I cannot but think there is no criminality on either side. CRIMINALITY! There is is a bar, at which those who dare to stigmatize an honest zeal in the cause of humanity as a crime, may find in their need as little mercy as they have been inclined to shew to their fellow-creatures, during their *little brief authority* in this vale of woe.

CRIMINALITY in wishing to terminate the calamity of war! On such a charge, I address not venal societies, interested courtiers, sneaking placemen, pensioners, expectants; but you, ye widows and ye orphans; you, ye poor mangled brethren; you also, ye PALE DEPARTED CORPSES! and, though I speak to cold and senseless ears when I speak to *you*; yet your blood cries to high heaven for mercy to mankind, and pleads powerfully, and, I hope, successfully, to those of your fellow creatures who have it in their power, to say, in the commanding language of the scriptures, " O THOU " SWORD, HOW LONG WILL IT BE ERE " THOU BE QUIET? PUT UP THYSELF " INTO THY SCABBARD; REST, AND BE " STILL\*." Slain ere ye had tasted the sweets of life, even in the early morning of your day, the flinty heart of *avarice* regards

\* Jer. xlvii. 6.

you not, *ambition* is too much engaged, and *vanity* too selfish to feel for any but itself; but RELIGION shall shed a tear over you, and daily pour her orison, that your few and evil days in this world may be compensated by a happiness where love shall reign, and war shall be no more.

But I must desist. Yet not till I have made my final declaration. I profess myself one who thinks war, offensive war, at once detestable, deplorable, and ridiculous. I profess myself the friend of the people, the friend of all mankind, in all countries, and of all colours; the low as well as the high, the high as well as the low; it is enough that they are fellow-men, alike born, alike to die; all of them, however distinguished for a few short years, doomed to mortality, like myself, and subject to the thousand miseries flesh is heir to;—to all of them, and not to any little party, *excluding all others* from love and mercy, I avow myself, in all that I ever preached and wrote, the disinterested friend; and when I cease to be so, may God Almighty palsy this tongue that has pleaded their cause with energy, and wither this hand which has often

written

written in their service; and which, for that reason alone, is now compelled to hold the pen in defence of myself and those I love, from envy, hatred, and anger, studiously fostered and disseminated by *invisible agents*, who, not content with a public insult, add to it, for its palliation in the eyes of others, *private obloquy*. It is observed, by those that have studied human nature, that they are the least inclined to forgive who committed the wrong. Then let me have the honour and happiness of freely forgiving *them*, who insulted *me* and *mine* unlawfully, indecently, and without cause. I do forgive them. I know not one of them; no, not even by name. I desire not to expose them. For me they are sheltered safely in their retirements. I wish them a merry Christmas in their winter-quarters, wherever they may be. May their mirth, at that happy season of love and friendship, be uninterrupted by DREAMS OF DEMOCRATS, and may they never have to encounter more dangerous foes than such as they have been used to engage and put to flight; SUPPOSED ENEMIES, on the Downs, and in the Theatre of Brighton.

# APPENDIX.

### N° I.

*A Letter from the Rev. Mr.* MOSSOP, *Curate of Brighton, who officiated in the Desk on the 18th of August, and was present during the whole of my Sermon. The Rev. Mr.* HUDSON, *the Vicar, was absent on that day; otherwise, I have no doubt but that he would have borne a similar testimony.*

Rev. Sir,

FROM my situation in the church at Brighthelmstone the day you favoured us with a sermon, which gave such high offence to a certain description of *gentlemen*, I have, as may naturally be supposed, had my ears sufficiently stunned with inquiries relative to this sermon, both by many that were *present*, as well as *absent*. From some of the former, I have experienced no small portion of ill-nature, because *I could not conscientiously join in the cry* with those who can judge the motives of their neighbour better than he can himself, and pronounce it at once seditious, libellous, traitorous, democratic.

The

The answer I have given to the latter description of inquirers, was in substance, "That I doubted "not but that Dr. Knox would submit his sermon, "in proper time, to that Public at large, which is "better able to judge, and generally more can- "did, than interested individuals, who often mis- "apprehend, but more frequently misrepresent, a "subject, to apologize for *illiberality and male- *volence*;*" adding, "That that christian cha- "rity, which men of our order ought to entertain "one towards another, would not allow me to "suppose, that Dr. Knox's motive was to hint, "in the most distant manner, at the subversion "of our present happy constitution and govern- "ment, but merely to expatiate on the advantages "of universal peace and goodwill among man- "kind, and to reprobate the decision of disputes "by the umpirage of the sword."

May I, therefore, take the liberty to ask, Whe- ther you have it in intention to publish the ser- mon, or not? that I may have an opportunity of gratifying my inquirers with a more satisfactory answer. As I am partly a stranger to you, I beg you will excuse this liberty; and remain,

  Rev. Sir,

    Your obedient humble servant,

      J. MOSSOP.

Brighthelmstone,
12th September 1793.

*To the Rev. Dr. Knox.*

N. B. *I never had the pleasure of speaking to this gentleman. I am totally unacquainted with him. From a pure love of justice and truth he sent me the above unexpected and unsolicited letter. On my asking his leave to publish it, he returned the following answer. It may be doubted whether certain* pluralists *and* court divines *would have dared to give so* honest *a testimony.*

---

## N° II.

Rev. Sir,

I DULY received yours of the 17th instant; and as I look upon you to be misrepresented to the Public, relative to the sermon you preached at Brighton, and consequently loaded with no small degree of unmerited opprobrium, I shall willingly contribute my mite to exonerate you. You have, therefore, my permission to publish my letter to you of the 12th of September last, in your intended vindication; provided your publication contain no invectives against the present existing government, nor any sentiments which might be improper for one zealously attached to our most excellent constitution to countenance.

I must conclude, by saying, that if every clergyman is to be exposed to insult, for doing what he conceives to be his duty, in expofing the reigning vices of the age, we fhall foon find, that the feeble rays of religion, which yet remain, to enlighten the chriftian world, will foon become totally eclipfed. I am,

    Rev. Sir,

        Your obedient humble fervant,

                J. MOSSOP.

BRIGHTHELMSTONE,
19th *November* 1793.

*To the Rev. Dr.* KNOX.

N. B. *Mr. Moffop's candour does him the more honour, as his ftipend confifts of the voluntary fubfcription of the* RICH, *who refort to Brighton; and as* GREAT PERSONAGES, *with their* tradefmen *and* retinue, *are among his parifhioners.*

---

## N° III.

My Dear Sir,

YOUR laft favour has found me fo much indifpofed by the rheumatifm, that it is not without effort I can acknowledge the receipt of your letter.

It will of courfe be out of my power to bear my teftimony in the way you mention, againft the

the extension of military controul over our places of diversion, our temples, and our altars; yet the more I reflect on the insult you received at Brighton, the greater is my concern, that a precedent of a nature so highly dangerous, should be permitted, by those in power, to pass uncensured and unpunished.

Since the men of the sword have dared to violate, not only the laws of decency, but those of their country, in your case, I cannot meet a cockaded stripling in his regimentals, or a foot soldier in the street, without feeling that we have masters, whose servants we are, although our estates and our industry are mortgaged to pay them their wages.

We shall perceive what the country will say and do when your Narrative is published.

If the hirelings of the pen are bidden to support those of the sword, by the persons who direct both, the matter is settled, and you are only the first victim. I am,

 My Dear Sir,
  with much esteem,
   Your faithful friend and servant,
        R. S.

LONDON,
Nov. 20, 1793.

## Nº IV.

Sir,

OUR excellent laws have guarded us from the assaults of malice, and of superior force, with peculiar care. The following quotations from JUDGE BLACKSTONE, with many others, will evince, that the greatest men, even ARMED, as your assailants were, and superior in numbers, *dare not*, consistently with a regard for our admirable constitution, attack the most defenceless member of the community. Yet your assailants, *in this very act*, pretended to be the defenders of the law and the constitution.

That learned judge, and friend to freedom and humanity, says, " Besides ACTUAL BREACHES of
" the peace, any thing that tends to provoke or
" excite others to break it, is an offence of the
" same denomination. Therefore challenges to
" fight, either by word or letter, or to be the bearer
" of such challenge, are punishable by fine and im-
" prisonment, according to the circumstance of the
" offence." Book IV. chap. 11. sect. 12.

" An *unlawful assembly* is when *three or more*
" do assemble themselves together to do an *un-*
" *lawful act*."——(☞ There was a CONSPIRACY of MANY more than three, *for two hours, against you*, in the Theatre, *assembled to do an* UNLAWFUL ACT; and they did it. *Hireling newspapers* defended

fended it; the readers of which PAY TWICE to be *deceived*; first the *wages*, then the price of the papers!)

"A RIOT is where three or more do an unlaw-
"ful act of violence, either *with* or without a
"*common cause of quarrel*; as if they beat a man,
"or *do any other unlawful act*, with force or vio-
"lence; or even do a *lawful act*, as REMOVING
"A NUISANCE, in a *violent and tumultuous* man-
"ner."       Book IV. chap. 11. sect. 6.

"The punishment of *unlawful assemblies*, from
"the number *three to eleven*, is fine and impri-
"sonment; if they amount to the number twelve,
"it may be CAPITAL."      BLACKSTONE.

"There is one species of battery more atro-
"cious and penal than the rest, which is the
"beating of a clerk in orders, or clergyman, on
"account of the respect and reverence due to
"his sacred character, as the MINISTER AND EM-
"BASSADOR OF PEACE."\*\*\*\*So that upon the
"whole it appears, that a person guilty of such
"*brutal* behaviour to a clergyman, is subject to
"three kinds of prosecution, all of which may
"be punished for one and the same offence; an
"indictment for the breach of the King's peace
"by such assault and battery; a civil action for
"the special damage sustained by the party in-
"jured; and a suit in the ecclesiastical court."

Book IV. chap. 15. sect. 7.

P                                          Every

Every REAL *Friend to our King and Constitution*, especially if by profession and solemn engagement bound to defend the country, and assist the civil power, in the suppression of riot, and the preservation of order, will himself be peculiarly careful not to break the law, and disturb the peace.

Judge Blackstone says, " All disturbances of " the peace, all OPPRESSIONS of a notoriously evil " example, may be indicted at the suit of the " KING." Book IV. chap. 15. sect. 8.

A code of laws which thus secures personal liberty to ALL, must be endeared to every Englishman who regards either himself or his fellow citizens.

" The least *touching* of another's person, wil- " fully or in anger, is a battery; for the law can- " not draw the line between different degrees of " violence, and therefore totally prohibits the first " and lowest stage of it; *every man's person* being " sacred, and no other having a right to meddle " with it, in any the slightest manner."
BLACKSTONE, Book III. chap. 8.

Would not one preach in defence of such a constitution, and pray too, saying, " Esto perpe- " tua !" Yes; though CLUB LAW and SWORD LAW should oppose THE LAW OF ENGLAND, *vi et armis*, let us all stand up, *as you have done*, advo-
cates

cates for it, and for our glorious constitution in its purity. I am, &c.

LEGULEIUS.

*P. S.* You remember a subject at College for a theme:

*Minor in prælio, non semper minor in causâ.*

I have just heard one of your assailants was a LITTLE LORD. He had a queer name of his own; but I cannot recollect it. I never knew before, that there was such a BEING in the universe.

---

## N° V.

Dear Sir,

WHEN you consider the great influence of enormous wealth, and its consequent power, *alarmed* at the rapid progress of *civil liberty*, you will cease to wonder at the indefatigable and successful exertions, which are made to crush individuals who publicly espouse its cause. No rancour is so venomous, as the rancour of wounded pride; of avarice, dreading the diminution of its revenues; of ambition, checked in its selfish and vain-glorious career. Nothing but a fear of the laws restrains a virulence so exasperated, from the most outrageous injustice. Reason, argument, persuasion, plead in vain against *irritated* tyranny.

Conscious power, goaded by *fear* and anger, hesitates at no villainous act of oppression, consistent with its own safety.

The ill-usage you have recently experienced, proves what military power, under *aristocratical* direction, would do, if it dared. Happily the laws still retain their vigour. Public spirit is not yet quite extinct. Englishmen will not yet suffer law and liberty to be trampled upon, with impunity.

I hope, therefore, that you will not be dispirited. I do assure you, that the silly calumnies of hired scribblers have done you no disservice among the *independent part* of the Public. They have only deceived those who were willing to be deceived; those who love to have their malevolence fed by a breakfast of paragraphs, equally replete with absurdity and virulence. A strange appetite! But calumny is as delightful food to some, as human flesh to tigers.

I have just this minute seen a paragraph in a paper, which I copy at the coffee-house, where I am now writing, for your amusement, while I drink my morning dish of tea.

After inveighing against you, the writer says, " The clergy have been accused, ere now, of in-
" dolence, of inability, of not taking the trouble
" even of writing their own discourses; but, my God!
" if these are the samples of them (meaning your
" sermon)

"sermon) when they do write, MAY THEY NEVER
"RESUME THE PEN! and we readily admit their
"old plea, "That the body of divinity now pub-
"lished, is already large enough to answer every
"purpose, if well inculcated."

But what, say I, should we do for sermons on the *thirtieth of January*, and on fast days, if the prayer of this writer should be heard, and the clergy *never resume the pen?* I suppose the DIGNIFIED part of them may *write* AGAINST the *people*; or why are they loaded with sinecures?

He adds, "The learned Doctor possesses great
"merit: How much to be wished it were dis-
"played in a BETTER CAUSE."

A better cause than the promotion of peace and good-will! These things are very diverting. I hope you laugh at them all. I am,

Sir,

Your humble servant,

CLERICUS.

FLEET-STREET,
Sept. 17, 1793.

*P. S.* I can contradict the report, that the Prince was AT CHURCH when you preached peace. He has a great number of *chaplains*; and, doubtless, hears divine service performed at the PAVILION. I wish he *had* been *at church*; he would, I am sure, have approved your doctrine, and reprimanded the military inquisition.

N° VI.

# Nº VI.

Sir,

In the 151st page of Mr. Burke's Reflections, which some of the aristocracy read with more devotion than the scriptures, we find it thus written:

"The Christian statesmen of this land are sen-
"sible, that *religious instruction* is of *more conse-*
"*quence* to the GREAT, *than any others*, from
"the necessity of bowing down the STUBBORN
"NECK of their pride and ambition, to the yoke
"of moderation and virtue; from a consideration
"of the FAT STUPIDITY and GROSS IGNORANCE
"*concerning what it imports men most to know*,
"which prevails at COURTS, and at the HEAD
"OF ARMIES, and in SENATES, *as much* (mark
"that!) as at the loom and in the field."

I think you must have Mr. Burke on your side, if he preserves his consistency. But what will your military antagonists say to him, when they read this? They will be tempted to hustle him in the lobby of the House of Commons, if he goes on in this strain. I heard your sermon. You said nothing so *offensive* to COURTS, or HEADS OF ARMIES, as this. Only consider the expressions:—" STUBBORN NECK—FAT STUPIDITY—GROSS

GROSS IGNORANCE." I think this paffage does Mr. Burke more honour, than all his flimfy wire-drawn ftuff, his fophiftical, paffionate, and romantic declamation againft human nature. *O fi fic omnia!*

But, for the life of me, when I read of *ftubborn neck*, FAT ftupidity, and *grofs ignorance*, I cannot help thinking of SWINE. Sure he does not mean to rank *People at Courts*, at the *Head of Armies*, and in *Senates*, with the fwinifh multitude. Yet he muft, when he attributes to them ftubborn necks, fat ftupidity, and grofs ignorance. It is to his honour, if he numbers the *rich and great vulgar* with the poor and abject. Truth will break forth. There are as many fwine, very FAT indeed with ftupidity, and with ftubborn necks, in gilded, and painted, and carved *ftyes*, as in ftyes covered with thatch, and fcarcely keeping off the pelting of the pitilefs ftorm. Bravo! Mr. Burke! This compenfates for a good deal of your abufe of thofe of your fellow creatures, whofe *crime is poverty*.

I have a notion Mr. Burke, confiftently with the above excellent paffage, would number *your affailants* with the SWINISH MULTITUDE. Not that he ventured to tell them fo, when he went to fee the " pride, pomp, and circumftance of " glorious war," on the *South Downs*. However, I am pretty fure he would not approve of your being *trodden down under the hoofs of a fwinifh multitude*.

*multitude*, for endeavouring, as he expresses it, to bow down the *stubborn neck* of pride and ambition, and to remove a little of that *fat stupidity* and *gross ignorance* which HE says, though *you* did not say, "*prevails even at the* HEAD OF "ARMIES."

The *swinish multitude* of *high life* are well described by Horace, in these celebrated words:

*Pinguem et nitidum, et bene curata cute porcum.*

I wish the poor *little* pigs were as fat and well-liking. May they never lack warm styes and full troughs!

I congratulate you on having so eloquent an advocate on your side as Mr. Burke.

He says in another place, a little lower down, "Our provident CONSTITUTION has taken care, "that those who are to instruct PRESUMPTUOUS "IGNORANCE, those who are to be censors over "INSOLENT VICE, should never incur their con- "tempt, nor live upon their alms." You see he stands up for the freedom and dignity of the pulpit.

These sentiments certainly do him honour. It is a pity that his grains of wheat are hidden in bushels of chaff, and his jewels lost in a dunghill. The SWINE, however, will rout them out.

That

That expression of "Swinish Multitude," was an unlucky *lapsus linguæ*.—But if we are swine, *Quid vetat et nosmet* grunnire? I am,

  Sir,

   Yours, &c.

  PINGUICULUS PORCELLUS.

---

## N° VII.

*[The following Account, though certainly founded on a conversation which actually passed at a public place, in the hearing of a person whose name I know, is probably intended to represent the spirit of the Tattlers upon this occasion.]*

Sir,

I was lately sitting in a snug corner in a bookseller's shop, at a place of public resort, when I was an eye and ear witness to the following scene and dialogue, which I take the liberty of transmitting to you for your edification.

*Enter six men, some with skirts to their coats, and some (exposing the seat of honour) without skirts; some with caps, and some with hats;*

hats; *some with feathers, and some with none; but all fierce of physiognomy, loud of voice, and (in course) desperately courageous.*

*1st.* D——n you, you Sir; did you hear the famous seditious sermon?

*2d.* No—*I hear it, aye? I never go to church. I* want to hear none of their GAB, not *I*; though I know all about it as well as if I had been there. But hold your jaw. I am reading the papers.—Good God! what a sad thing it is; the French I see are all turned atheists. They have abolished Sundays, and discarded their clergy. I hope to God we shall exterminate the banditti;—a pack of Sans Culottes and Carmagnols.

*1st.* But this sermon runs in my head. It was full of treason and sedition. It was all about feathers, and sword-knots, and epaulettes. But one comfort is—I hear the preacher is taken up.

*3d.* Yes he is, and I hope he will be taken down. What do you think he said, you? Why he said—*(hah, hah, he!)* he said—All mankind are brothers—Brothers! *hah, hah, he!* Lady Proudflesh, who you know is a lady of family and the first fashion, told me she thought she should have burst her sides a laughing at the idea. It is *too* bad. I am told a prosecution is commenced.

*4th.* It is, it is.—What's as bad—he told the men not to mind the officers a skip of a louse—that was

his

his expreſſion. I know a man that will take his bible oath of it. Then he went on and ſaid—They ought to bid the colonel kiſs their breeches. He uſed plainer Engliſh. Well; that was not all. He ſaid, You Sirs, ſays he, addreſſing himſelf to the men, you are a pack of fools, ſays he, and your commanders are all knaves and ſycophants. The whole army was there—there was not a man left in the camp—all at the church; and they no ſooner came out, than they fell a mutinying like mad. D—n it, ſays I; ſo I ups with my ſword, and runs a dozen of them through the body at a thruſt; with one foot I kicked a ſcore over the cliff; with the other, I ſent a little hundred into the clay-pits belonging to the brick-kiln; and with my left hand I collared a dozen more; and then they all marched back as quiet as lambs, and no more was heard of the mutiny.

5*th*. I ſaw you, I ſaw you do it, by G—; and Tim Figgins, of the Gothamſhire, ſays he was one of the mutineers; for he heard the parſon ſay, On earth peace. That was all he heard; but a comrade of his told him, peace was proclaimed in the Goſpel Gazette; and that we were all to go home, and take care of our families, and plough the ground for the next wheat harveſt: So he was ſkipping about for joy, but meant no harm, when you attacked him in the rear with your foot, and laid him ſprawling on the beach. By G—, the parson ought to be brought to a court martial though.

*6th.* He will, he will. But you have not heard *half.* The sermon was the most flagitious, factious, seditious, traiterous, libellous, mutinous, villainous, rascally, scoundrelly sermon that ever was preached in a pulpit, by G—. Lady Epaulette told me he actually described the pattern of the cotton lining of the prince's tent, and held out a yard or two for every body to see it, and said, What a shame! No wonder the national debt has increased to such an enormous pitch. Lady Epaulette reddened so at church, you could not tell the difference between the colour of her face and her regimentals, by G—. Lady Bumfidget was so mad she could have cried, but she turned it off to a laugh, and patted the captain on the shoulder a hundred times, while he bit his lips and vowed vengeance. Too bad! too bad! said old Mrs. Tattle, our landlady. But *he* went on talking about peace and war. Now that I do not mind so much. Damn all he said about stopping the effusion of blood. *If he had stuck to peace, damn it, we should not have minded that* [*]. But feathers! If I do not revenge.—What do you think he had the impudence to say? Why—fine feathers make fine birds. That was the worst of all. D—n all his other sedition. That galls me.

[*] One of the *party engaged* said this repeatedly in the Play-House Lobby, during the action.

*1st.* And

1*st*. And *me* too.
2*d*. *I* don't like *that*.
3*d*. No!—Any thing but *that*.
4*th*. *I* feel hurt at *that*.
5*th*. Aye, *there*'s the rub.
6*th*. " *The time and the place make it criminal.*"

A grave old gentleman, who had sat with a stick in his hand, gently tapping his shining boots all this while, now rose, and respectfully asked the 1st, Pray, Sir, were you present at the sermon. He proceeded to ask them all in order.

Answer 1*st*. No—but I am credibly informed of all its contents by my laundress, who had it from Lady Van Helmet's waiting-maid, whom she went to drink tea with that very Sunday evening; so she must remember it all perfectly.

2*d*. A very respectable man, who has a very good place under Government, told me, and he had it from a cousin of one of our contractors, who heard it from an old deaf woman that sat in the church porch all the while, from the text to the blessing. A very honest creature—he gave her a halfpenny for her intelligence, and she promised to bring him some more.

3*d*. I gave sixpence to a soldier's wife, that mends stockings for me, to tell me all about it. I am afraid the hussey cheated me; for I asked her what sort of a man the preacher was, and she said

he

he wore a ... wig, and preached in spectacles— which, I am told, is not the case; but, however, the poor woman might make use of her ears, though not her eyes. Her account tallies, in other respects, with all the rest; and I have no doubt she will make affidavit of it, for she spoke very confidently, and she is wretchedly poor. I have not paid her bill for some time.

*4th.* My grandmother was there; and my nephew Jack, it seems, caught her napping in the pew, as fast asleep as a church, and gave her a good smart tweak by the nose, without waking her. He told her of it as soon as she came home. But the old lady proved she was wide awake, by repeating the Creed and the *Catechize,* from one end to the other. She forgot the text, I believe— but she said she remembered the sermon well, vowed it was all treason, and poor Jack got a box on the ear for his pains.

*5th.* I went out to tea that afternoon. None of us knew a word about the sermon; till Mr. Bustle entered in a hurry, and said, one of the messengers had just arrived and apprehended the preacher. All the company stared; and knowing nothing of the sermon, asked the footboy, who had leave to go to church in the morning, but who, it seems, had gone to see the two men hanging in chains hard by. He slips out to fetch some toast, and inquires of Dorothy, the cook in the kitchen, who happening to have company herself, found out from the washer-woman, that the preacher pulled the Prince's tent to pieces, and said we were all brothers and sisters. Lord-a-mercy! says she,—I be sister to a prince! and old Smoaker his brother! If that ben't treason, I do not know what is. I hope the parson will be taken up. I'll peach him; they say a body may make a penny of it. She is rather hard of hearing, but an honest good creature, and I intend to take her words down, and insert them in the Lying Advertiser, or the False Briton.

Answer the sixth.

I had my intelligence from my valet de chambre, who had it from his maiden aunt that had a dream. She thought she saw all the Sans Culottes, in their miserable uncloathed condition, upon the beach, which frightened her into fits. Whereupon she went to tell it to an acquaintance of hers, the wife of a man who has a snug place in the India-House; and she, it seems, was at the church. Upon hearing her story of treason and sedition, the old soul was at no loss to account for her dream. It seems the good woman, who had *heard* the sermon, came home highly pleased, and was wishing for peace, when her husband interrupted, and says, Jenny, says he, take care what you say. I hear it was all treason. You must take t'other side of the question, my dear. True, says she. Aye, a nod's as good as a wink; a word to the wife. " Now, " Jenny,

"  Jenny, can't you recollect any little bit of trea-
" son, Jenny, just to tell the captain?"—" O yes,"
says she, " I believe I can, for that matter."—" Well
" then let's have it."—" Why he said something
" that tends immediately *to the subversion of the*
" *government.*"—" Did he so? did he so? that's
" good—so much the better—very well indeed—
" let's have it—What did he say, my dear?"—
" Why he said, That we ought, all of us, to be
" GOVERNED by—yes, he said GOVERNED—mark
" that—take that down—*governed* by one PHIL.
" ANTHROPY. I do not know who Philip is—
" some outlandish prince or Sans Culotte or ano-
" ther—but whether he be the pope, the devil, or
" the pretender, I will take my bible oath, before
" any justice of peace, that he said we ought to be
" governed by one Phil. Anthropy; whereas, you
" know, we have no right to be governed but by
" the existing government. There we have him.
" This will make interest with *somebody* you know.
" Aye, aye—No Phil. Anthropy. No Philan-
" thropy, say I. No strangers. No philanthropy."

The old gentleman smiled and said, I find you
were none of you present at the sermon. Now I
was there; and I affirm that it was, from beginning
to end, calculated to serve the cause of humanity,
and no other cause. You have been misled by the
silly tales of the idle, the interested, and the wicked.
*All.*

*All.* " Who are you?—who are you?"

An ENGLISHMAN. A MAN. I wear no sword indeed; but I have a tongue to contradict a liar, and a good staff of ENGLISH OAK to defend myself against a ruffian. Here is my address. I will convince you of your error, if you will listen to reason.

*All.* " Reason? Oh, we have nothing to do with
" it—it is nothing to us."

[*Exeunt—sneaking and muttering.*

*1st.* A d——d Quiz this.

*2d.* A queer put.

*3d.* An old curmudgeon.

*4th.* A son of a b—.

*5th.* A democratical rascal.

*6th.* I, I, I don't half like him—O, here he comes—Why did not you knock him down, Jack?

*1st.* I'll teach him to jaw, if I ever meet him again.

*2d.* I had a good mind to draw my sword.

*3d.* I had my hand upon the hilt of mine.

*4th.* If he had not stopt his *slang*, I'd have *pinked* him, or I'll be shot.

*5th.* I would have kicked his ——.

*6th.* I wish he was here now—I, I, I, I—O Lord, here he comes—good morning—let's go. Devil take the old democrat, say I.—No democrats. I'm off.—Damme, I don't like democrats with *staves of English oak*, not I.—*Good morning to you, Sir.* [*Exeunt omnes.*

The old gentleman took a pinch of snuff, and coolly walked up and down the promenade. Yours,

DEMOCRITUS.

*P. S.* I hear the angry warriors *actually met* to concert measures for *prosecuting* you; but *no two of them could agree in the same story.* So they damned one another, and parted. It seems, it was a little JEW that called from his box for *personal injury.* He was as arbitrary as if he had been his most CHRISTIAN Majesty, for whom your *true-bred English patriot* would fight the devil.

## N° VIII.

Sir,

I AM an officer; and though I did not hear your sermon, yet I can readily believe it was full of treason, from one end to the other. I know it was. I do not often read sermons; but upon hearing of your treason, I determined to look into your *volume of sermons,* which you published two or three years ago, in the hope of finding something to convict you, if my brother officers should unluckily have forgotten the worst parts of that flagitious discourse at Brighton. I could find nothing myself, but some old-fashioned doctrines about faith, hope, and charity. But my good friend Doctor Plumpton, having nothing to do on Sundays, (as he keeps three curates, at thirty pounds a-year each, and his

his ftall is a finecure,) employed one whole Sunday morning in endeavouring to find out fome treafon in your fermons. And, fure enough, here it is. The Doctor fent it me in a frank, given him by the member for the borough, who got him all his preferment. The Doctor fays he cannot fee (though he wears fpectacles too) what in the world the Public can find in your foolifh books to buy them. He himfelf has favoured the Public with one whole fermon, on " SUBMISSION TO THE POWERS " THAT BE," and he never got rid of any, but thofe that he prefented in Turkey leather, gilt and lettered, to the Minifter, and a few of the *letter fort*. But to the *treafon*. This will *do* for you, Sir. Here it is, in page 377, of your fecond edition. Mrs. Plumpton copied it for the Doctor, as writing is fatiguing to him, efpecially after dinner. I have not read it; but I dare fay your *diocefan* will make you an example for it. I hope to God he may.

" Such, indeed, is the violence of political
" animofity, that every focial Chriftian duty is
" facrificed to the indulgence of it: hatred of the
" bitterest kind is occafioned by a difference in
" politics, or by an attachment to a favourite
" ftatefman, or fyftem of public conduct; and it
" is greatly to be lamented that this violence of
" zeal arifes not from the pure motives of genuine
" patriotifm, to which it arrogantly pretends, but
" from envy, from a contentious temper, from
" vanity, from ambition.

" I moft

"I moſt earneſtly admoniſh all who are inſtigated by theſe motives to ſeditious language, writing, or action, to conſider that they are inſulting the King of Kings, who delights in order and tranquillity, and whoſe gracious goſpel particularly requires a peaceful ſubmiſſion to the laws of a country, and to the powers legally eſtabliſhed. Confuſion, and every evil work, are the conſequences of the unruly paſſions of envy and ſtrife, when they direct their force againſt the civil government and its proper adminiſtrators. *Fear God and honour the King*, are commands joined together in the ſcriptures ſo cloſely, as to induce one to conclude, that to honour the King is to perform a duty at leaſt approaching to the nature of a religious office. But if this ſhould not be allowed, yet it is certainly true, that to diſturb any good government is contrary to the duty of a good man, and particularly inconſiſtent with the character of a good Chriſtian, who ſhould ſtudy to be quiet, and to mind his own buſineſs, and not to follow thoſe who, from *envy and ſtrife*, are given to *unneceſſary* innovation."

I ſay I have not read it myſelf; but I take Doctor Plumpton's word for it. He *looked* very angry with you. So he judges fairly. He hates you worſe than the devil. So he is impartial.

I thought it but fair to let you know before-hand what I intend to proſecute you for; ſo have taken

this

this trouble, which, by the way, is doing you more honour than you deferve. You know they told you your deferts. *A la lanterne*, fhould have been the word. They *did imitate* the *French very well.*

I wifh I had been in the Theatre. I am told they had not men enough, or that enterprize would have turned out ftill more glorious than it did, though it did them all honour.

Good fubjects ought to be diftinguifhed; and, therefore, I hope fome *ribbons* will be beftowed on the moft active of thofe good men, who proved, on that occafion, that they do not degenerate from the Wolfes and the Marlboroughs that adorn our Englifh hiftory. I am glad to fee the good old bulldog breed kept up. Let's have no more of your fnivelling about peace. What fhould you know about peace or war? Leave every one to his own bufinefs, fay I; and don't let the cobler go beyond his laft.

There's Dean Swift now, I like *him*. I accidentally opened one of his books t'other day, and my eye fell on the following paffage. The affair happened at a coffee-houfe.

An *officer*, you muft know, in company with a *clergyman*, had a little difpute. But the Doctor met with his match, by God.

You fhall judge. You fhall hear Dean Swift's own words. " D—n me, Doctor," (cried the officer,) " fay what you will, the army is the only *fchool* for
" gene

"gentlemen. Do you think my Lord Marlborough
"beat the French with Greek and Latin? D—n
"me, I would be glad, by G—d, to see any of
"your scholars, with his nouns and his verbs, and
"his philosophy and his trigonometry, what a
"figure he would make at a siege, or blockade,
"or rencountering!" The parson had nothing to
say.

So you see the affair at Brighton is not the first in which the officers were too many for the parson. I only wish I had been there, that's all. It was an additional feather in the cap of all the parties, male and female, concerned therein. That's poz.

None of yours, by G—d,

B——Y DAWSON.

BULL AND MOUTH STREET,
  *Aug.* 25, 1793.

*P. S.* Damn you, I'll fight you, if you'll come without your children to take your part. Not else;—five or six to one's odds, by G—.

---

## N° IX.

Rev. Sir,

I was lately in company with some *professional* gentlemen and their ladies, when the comical pranks of the military at Brighton Theatre became the topic of conversation. One of them said he heard you intended to *prosecute* your assailants;

upon

upon which they all burst out into a loud laugh, declaring, they never heard any thing more diverting in their lives. Prosecute, indeed ! said a smart martinet. I say prosecute too, cried an emaciated lady in a *helmet*, at the same time pursing up her mouth, and fanning away most rapidly. " What's " that?" asked a veteran who had been whistling " What can the matter be?" while he adjusted his frill with one hand, and beat time on the ivory hilt of his sword with the other. " What's that? "Does he say he will prosecute? Never believe " it. He knows better than to prosecute. Their " PURSES ARE A LITTLE TOO HEAVY FOR HIM, " my dear." Here he winked his eye; and they all joined with an air of triumph, and repeated; Yes, yes,—Their PURSES ARE A LITTLE TOO HEAVY FOR HIM. I do assure you this is *literally true*; and from it I conclude, that these heroic souls imagined that

> Offence's gilded hand might shove by *justice*,
> But 'tis not so in ENGLAND.—

By the way, you should not have preached the Gospel of peace before men who *live* by war. Truth is not to be told at all times. Never preach the Gospel when it may give offence, or obstruct your preferment. Preach about any thing that is not interesting, and does not come home to men's business and bosoms. Be as dull you please; you will be safe. Apropos, I met with the following

lowing passages from a shrewd author, who wrote about fifty years ago. Read; and learn to preach the *right way*, do; make the pulpit a *drum ecclesiastic*. *That's your sort* to please.

"Whenever pillage or shedding of blood are to be justified or encouraged by a sermon, or men are to be exhorted to a battle, to the sacking of a city, or the destruction of a country, by a pathetic discourse, the *text* is always taken from the OLD TESTAMENT. ('*War*' *Gospel!*)

"But to make it evident, that divines may be useful to all fighting men, without preaching of the *Gospel*, we need but to consider, that among all the wars and dissensions which *Christians* have had one with another, there never was a cause yet so unreasonable or absurd, so unjust or openly wicked, if it had an *army to back it*, that has not found *christian divines*, or at least such as stiled themselves so, who have espoused and called it RIGHTEOUS. No rebellion was ever so unnatural, nor TYRANNY so CRUEL, but if there were men who would fight for it, there were priests who would pray for it, and loudly maintain that it was THE CAUSE OF GOD." *Dialogues on Honour*, page 159.

* * * * * * * * *

"However,

"However, morality is often preached to them,
"and even the GOSPEL, at SEASONABLE times,
"when they are in winter quarters, or in an idle
"summer, when there is no enemy near, and the
"troops are encamped in a country where no
"hostilities can be committed. But when they
"are to enter upon action, to besiege a large
"town, or ravage a rich country, it would be
"very *impertinent* to talk to them of their *christian*
"*virtues*, DOING AS THEY WOULD BE DONE BY,
"LOVING THEIR ENEMIES, and EXTENDING THEIR
"CHARITY TO ALL MANKIND. NOT A WORD OF
"THE GOSPEL, nor of meekness and humility.
"All thoughts of CHRISTIANITY are *laid aside*
"entirely. The men are praised and buoyed up
"in the high value they have for themselves.
"Their officers call them gentlemen and fellow-
"soldiers. Generals pull off their hats to them;
"and no artifice is neglected that can flatter
"their pride, or inspire them with a LOVE OF
"GLORY!

"The clergy themselves take care at such
"times not to mention to them their sins, or
"any thing that is melancholy or disheartening.
"On the contrary, they speak chearfully to them;
"encourage and *assure them* of God's favour.
"They take pains to justify, and endeavour to
"INCREASE THE ANIMOSITIES and AVERSION
"which those under their care have against their
"enemies,

"enemies, whom, to BLACKEN and RENDER
"ODIOUS, they leave no art untried, no stone
"unturned; and NO CALUMNY can be more ma-
"licious, no story more incredible, nor falsity
"more notorious, than have been made use of,
"knowingly, for that purpose, by *christian di-
"vines*, both protestants and papists." *Dialogues on Honour,* page 162.

 I am, Rev. Sir, with the greatest respect,
   Your obedient humble servant,
       T. B.

PORTSMOUTH,
*Sept.* 21, 1793.

 P. S. I observed you ended your sermon with a benevolent prayer. Take care not to pray too ardently for enemies. And, I beseech you, don't let the Reverend Dr. Par be your model in prayers; for these are his words; you may read them in his *Sequel*, page 73.

 " If," says that learned and able Divine, " the
" *threatened crusade* of RUFFIAN DESPOTS should
" be attempted, it will, in my opinion, be an out-
" rageous infringement upon the law of nations;
" it will be a SAVAGE CONSPIRACY against the
" written and unwritten rights of mankind; and,
" therefore, in the *sincerity of my soul*, I PRAY the
" righteous Governor of the universe, the Creator
" of men, and the King of kings, I PRAY him to
" abate the pride, assuage the malice, and con-
         " found

"found the devices of all parties, directly or in-
"directly leagued in this complicated scene of guilt
"and horror! this insult upon the dignity of hu-
"man nature itself! this treason against the MA-
"JESTY of God's own image, rational and immor-
"tal MAN."

There's a fervent prayer for you! but take heed how you pray in like manner, in the hearing of the said RUFFIAN DESPOTS. Luckily the ocean rolls between them and us; so that though they probably have LONG EARS, as you know they have proverbially LONG HANDS, yet they could not hear Dr. Par, especially as the cannon were roaring, and the drums were beating, and the dying were *howling*, for many leagues together.

## N° X.

Sir,

I AM very angry; very angry indeed. In the newspaper account of the Brighton outrage, I read that *military* men did so and so. *Military* men! *military* men, *Sir!* I tell you it is not true, Sir. Depend upon it—they were foxhunters in red coats, with a pack of puppies yelping at their heels; but no *military* men. We, Sir, know better. There is not a set of more generous men on God's earth than the military. I, for my part, would

would as soon attack my own father and mother, as insult a woman, or threaten a clergyman, especially when I was *armed*, assisted with a numerous body, and personally unprovoked. Blood and oons, Sir! I tell you once more, the military are incapable of such an action. You do not know the names or qualities of the party concerned; therefore you *may* be, and I say you *must* be, mistaken in thinking they were of the military order. A red coat don't make a soldier. A title is one thing, and honour another. I am only a SERJEANT, God knows; but I have got many an honourable scar, fighting face to face, in the field of battle. No man can say I ever thought my red coat and sword *privileged* me to affront women and children; and as to *calling names*, d—n me, (God forgive me for swearing;) but sooner than spit my spite by calling names, I would pull off my regimentals, and put on petticoats.

I am clear no military men were concerned. I wanted to set you right. So begging your honour's pardon for this freedom, I remain,

Sir,

Your humble servant,

JOHN SMITH,

*A Serjeant in the Regulars.*

STRAND, LONDON,
*Sept.* 20, 1793.

THE END.

www.ingramcontent.com/pod-product-compliance
Lightning Source LLC
Chambersburg PA
CBHW032158160426
43197CB00008B/967